PRAISE FOR *PRICELESS*

Every young person longs to feel secure and significant, and my friend
Jen Barrick understands. Even after a terrible accident left devastating
injuries, Jen held fast to the God of the Bible. And in Jen's new book,
Priceless, she leads other young people on a personal and power-
ful journey toward finding significance and security in the Lord.
You'll love it!

JONI EARECKSON TADA
Joni and Friends International Disability Center

Packed full of amazing wisdom, hope, and a lot of encouragement,
Priceless by my dear friend Jen Barrick is every young woman's
must-read devotional each and every day. She is an absolute treasure
from the Lord.

MEGAN ALLISON
Author of *Totally God's* and *Smart Girls, Smart Choices*

Jennifer Barrick authentically unveils the many issues of a teen girl's
heart and marvelously provides the Answer they all need by pointing
her audience toward an intimate relationship with Christ. *Priceless*
contains lifelong truths that are life-changing. This devotional book
is a must-read for any young woman in search of love and security.

MONICA ROSE BRENNAN
Director of the Center for Women's Leadership,
School of Divinity, Liberty University

I have traveled the world and met so many young women who need
what *Priceless* offers: a reminder that God has created them uniquely,
beautifully, and with intention. Jen's life is on display throughout
these pages, and it's clear that God has written her story to impact
and inspire this generation.

NOEL BREWER YEATTS
President, World Help

WHO I AM WHEN I FEEL . . .

JEN BARRICK *WITH* LINDA BARRICK

MOODY PUBLISHERS

CHICAGO

Edited by Annette LaPlaca
Cover design and lettering: Link Creative, Lindsey K.Meredith
Interior design: Erik M. Peterson and Julia Ryan (DesignByJulia.com)
Interior images: copyright © Shutterstock and illustrator unless stated otherwise:
    Metelitsa Viktoriya (Image# 376076176), Katya Bogina (Image# 259376189),
    Rudchenko Liliia (Image# 456094897).
Interior illustration of emoji in Day 14 copyright © 2018 by Cougarsan/
    Dreamstime.com (95553223). All rights reserved.
Author photo: Gaudium Photography

ISBN: 978-0-8024-1871-5

We hope you enjoy this book from Moody Publishers. Our goal is to
provide high-quality, thought-provoking books and products that
connect truth to your real needs and challenges. For more information
on other books and products written and produced from a biblical perspective,
go to www.moodypublishers.com or write to:

Moody Publishers
820 N. LaSalle Boulevard
Chicago, IL 60610

1 3 5 7 9 10 8 6 4 2

Printed in the United States of America

To every girl who has felt alone or unwanted.

You are a priceless treasure, a daughter of the King!

CONTENTS

Jen's Story 10

Day 1 When I Feel Like I'm **Not Enough** . . .
I'm Priceless *Psalm 36:5–9* 19

Day 2 When I Feel **Abandoned** . . .
I'm Wanted by God *Psalm 27:8–13* 27

Day 3 When I Feel **Afraid** . . .
I'm Fearless Because God Is with Me
Psalm 27:1–5 33

Day 4 When I Feel **Alone** . . .
I'm Surrounded by God *Psalm 139:5–10* 40

Day 5 When I Feel **Angry** . . .
I'm Trusting God to Defend Me *Psalm 37:4–9* 45

Day 6 When I Feel **Annoyed** . . .
I'm Free to Choose Thoughts That Please God
Psalm 19:12–14 52

Day 7 When I Feel **Ashamed** . . .
I'm Forgiven *Psalm 32:1–7* 58

Day 8 When I Feel **Awkward** . . .
I'm Confident in God's Love for Me
Psalm 57:2–10 63

Day 9 When I Feel **Beautiful** . . .
I'm Reflecting God's Glory *Psalm 45:7–11* 69

Day 10 When I Feel **Betrayed** . . .
I'm Giving My Burdens to God *Psalm 55:12–22* 76

Day 11 When I Feel **Confused** . . .
        I'm Guided by God *Psalm 37:23–24* 83

Day 12 When I Feel **Disappointed** . . .
        I'm Expecting God to Make a New Path
        Psalm 77:7–19 89

Day 13 When I Feel **Dumb** . . .
        I'm Wise in God's Eyes *Psalm 34:2–10* 95

Day 14 When I Feel **Embarrassed** . . .
        I'm Sheltered by God *Psalm 91:1–4, 9–11*. 103

Day 15 When I Feel **Excited** . . .
        I'm Grateful *Psalm 100:1–5* 109

Day 16 When I Feel **Fat** . . .
        I'm Just the Right Size for My Destiny
        Psalm 73:3–5, 21–28 114

Day 17 When I Feel **Invisible** . . .
        I'm Seen and Known *Psalm 33:13–23* 121

Day 18 When I Feel **Left Out** . . .
        I'm Chosen by God *Psalms 18:16–19; 94:14* 127

Day 19 When I Feel Like **Crying** . . .
        I'm Comforted by God *Psalms 56:8; 42:3–8*. 133

Day 20 When I Feel Like **Dancing** . . .
        I'm Making God Smile *Psalm 30:5–12* 140

Day 21 When I Feel Like **Giving Up** . . .
        I'm about to Be Rescued *Psalm 107:4–9*. 144

Day 22 When I Feel Like **Laughing** . . .
        I'm Praising God *Psalm 126:2–6* 150

Day 23 When I Feel **Like Singing . . .**
        I'm Energized *Psalm 96:1–4* 156

Day 24 When I Feel **Misunderstood . . .**
        I'm Heard by God *Psalm 17:1–7* 161

Day 25 When I Feel **Nervous . . .**
        I'm Victorious *Psalm 62:1–8* 168

Day 26 When I Feel **Stressed . . .**
        I'm Being Led to a Calmer Place *Psalm 23* 174

Day 27 When I Feel **Tempted . . .**
        I'm Too Valuable for Trouble *Psalm 141:3–10* 178

Day 28 When I Feel **Tired . . .**
        I'm Relying on God's Strength *Psalm 18:29–36* 183

Day 29 When I Feel **Ugly . . .**
        I'm Wonderfully Made *Psalm 139:13–18* 190

Day 30 When I Feel **Unpopular . . .**
        I'm Made to Stand Out *Psalm 138:1–8* 195

        A Personal Note from Jen 201

        Acknowledgments 203

JEN'S STORY

On the surface, my life was pretty good. At age fifteen, I worked hard to be a varsity cheerleader and varsity soccer player. I studied long hours to make the honor roll, sang in my high school choir, and had a boyfriend on the football team and a lot of really nice friends. Most importantly, I loved God with all of my heart. Every morning I set my alarm early so I could sit in my lime-green chair and read my Bible and pray. No doubt, God had given me just about everything a girl could want. There was only one thing missing: *boldness.* I passionately wanted to make a difference, to change the world, to tell others about how they could have a love relationship with Jesus, but I never knew quite how to get the words out. If only people could see what was really going on inside my head and heart. There was so much I wanted to say and share with people, but I was shy.

All of that changed in one second, the moment a drunk driver hit our car. My family and I were driving home one night in our minivan from my choir concert, when a full-size truck ran us over going eighty miles per hour with no headlights and no warning. I was in a coma for five weeks. When I woke up, everything was different. Because of a serious brain injury, I would never be able to cheer again

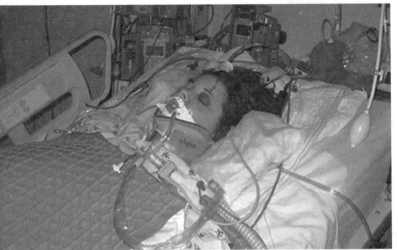

or play soccer. I'd never be able to drive a car. I had to relearn everything: walking, talking, eating. Most of my friends changed. My life changed. Even my personality was different.

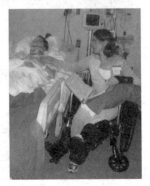

The only thing that didn't change was my love relationship with Jesus and my desire to tell people about Him. Before the accident, I had written a prayer to God in my private journal I kept under my bed. Here's what I asked:

Wow! It's crazy how time flies and years go by. Lord, this year I don't want to blend in because I know I was born to stand out. To stand alone? Maybe. If that is what it takes. This life I now live is not mine but Yours. Lord, pretty much I'm just begging You to take this year and my life and allow Your glory to shine. Take it and use it to its fullest potential. Father, I know You use the weak and incapable for Your glory, so that means You can use me just as I am. . . . Daddy, I know that together we can change the world.

Only God fully knew the desires and longing of my heart. I never dreamed He'd answer this prayer in such a dramatic way! My brain injury caused a lot of things to get "rewired" inside my head. Instead of being timid and shy, I said everything I thought or felt out loud. If I thought your outfit didn't match, I'd tell you right to your face. I would have never done that before! I'd also tell you how much Jesus loved you and wanted to have a personal relationship with you, without holding back anything. I was completely uninhibited, which made for some funny moments at times, but it answered the

prayer in my journal! It was as if God had opened the doors of my heart so others could see everything going on inside.

Now, more than ten years later, God has used my injury, my brokenness, and my new personality to give me a voice to girls all over the world. I would have never had the ability to do that with-

out first having the foundation of learning how to talk to God and, second, surrendering my life to His plan. My hope and prayer is that God will use this book to help you learn how to talk to Him, how to pour out the desires of your heart to Him in a two-way conversation, *where you know He hears you and talks back!* My other hope is that you will draw closer to Him and one step closer to discovering the amazing adventure He has planned for your life. He has something incredible planned that only you can do. You are special and one-of-a-kind! There is no one quite like you. I'm praying God will open the doors to your heart.

My HOPE for you ...

I know at your age you sometimes get labeled an "emotional roller coaster." You've probably heard people talk about how unstable your feelings are, and they probably weren't talking about them in a positive way. Maybe it almost made you feel like something was wrong with you or like you didn't have the freedom to be yourself. The surge of feelings you are experiencing right now are part of God's perfect design for you to get to know Him better. What if this age you are at right now isn't just an emotional roller coaster? What if it is the perfect age for you to learn to worship God with all your heart and soul because you are bubbling over with feelings? What if God planned this special time as you blossom into

adulthood to capture your whole heart because your heart is so full? I want you to know that I love your age. God loves your stage. He created and designed it for you to experience *more* of Him.

In a lot of ways, God "froze" me at fifteen. Because of my injury, I will always "feel" like a teenager in some ways. I also now say everything I feel out loud! This has given me a unique glimpse into the heart and needs of every teenage girl. I'll never forget one day hearing my mom say, "Oh my goodness, Jen, you constantly say out loud what every teenage girl is feeling but doesn't know how to put into words. We need to write a book to help girls understand what they are feeling."

And so . . . we did!

My mom would ask me about a feeling, and I would explain how we girls feel. Then we would take these feelings to the truth of God's Word. My mom would read me a Scripture, and I would pray the Scripture out loud back to God. All of this had to be recorded on my mom's iPhone because, girlfriend, I cannot write very fast anymore, and I can't always remember what I just said! My short-term memory is still a struggle, but God helps me do the impossible. Remember, I told you my brain injury changed a lot of things. You have to know it is a miracle that I could write a book. I can barely find my way to the bathroom sometimes.

God is healing me more and more every day. When I first woke up from the coma, I did not even recognize my family. I couldn't write my name, much less a book! I had lost a lot, but God miraculously preserved a lot too—including every praise song I'd ever learned. The

last thing I did before my accident was sing a song—a song that would be very special to me in the months ahead. It was all about the names of God and Him being my Best Friend! When you start waking up from a coma, you are very confused about who you are and where you are and how to do anything. That song would calm me down and help me feel the peace and  presence of God. My family would play it over and over in my hospital room to help me get through some very difficult days.

Right now you probably have some difficult days too. You may not have a brain injury, but you have a lot of changes to navigate. A lot is changing about your body, your feelings, your friends, and your life. I know it can be very overwhelming at times. Since it was a song that really helped me get through my years of drastic changes, I chose some songs to share with you. Did you know that God wrote you a bunch of songs? The whole book of Psalms is really just a collection of songs about all kinds of feelings. Each day, we'll look at a feeling and compare it to one of God's songs that will remind you how much He loves you and how beautiful and perfect you are in His eyes.

A few months ago I was standing in my bedroom, looking at myself in the mirror that hangs over my antique dresser. I just happened to be counting my scars. I was curious to find out how many I had left from my accident. I was feeling a little bothered by them. But the moment I figured out the number, it was like God whispering to my heart:

Jen, I don't look at you and think, oh, she's the girl with all the scars. No. When I look at you, I see that you are worth it.

You are priceless!

You are beautiful.

You are mine.

God feels the same way about you. When He looks at you, He doesn't see your brokenness. He sees your potential and what you will become with His strength. Your value can't be measured because you are *priceless*.

Let's start this adventure together!

Day 1

When I feel like I'm
NOT ENOUGH . . .
I'm *priceless*

WHO DO YOU THINK YOU ARE?

How would you describe yourself in three words?

1. _____

2. _____

3. _____

How would your friends or family describe you?
(Text somebody who knows you and ask him or
her to give you three words right now!)

1. _____

2. _____

3. _____

How do you think God would describe you in
three words?

1. _____

2. _____

3. _____

WHO ARE YOU REALLY?

- You are not who you think you are.

- You are not who others think you are.

- You are so much more than you may have ever imagined.

Let me explain.

God thinks you are valuable, but He also thinks you have fallen short of His high standards for heaven. Don't worry; everyone falls short of the perfect holiness of heaven (Rom. 3:23). But because God loves you so incredibly, crazy much, He made a way for you to become good enough for heaven. He sent His Son, Jesus, to trade places with you. He did all the work. You only have to receive His free gift of salvation by grace through faith (Eph. 2:8–9). That means believing what Jesus did on the cross to pay for your sins was enough to count for you. It's that simple.

Once you accept God's gift of salvation, you become one with Christ. If you are one with Christ, everything that is true about Christ is true about you. Second Corinthians 5:21 says, "God made him [Christ] who had no sin to be sin for us, so that in him we might become the righteousness of God" (NIV). When you become a follower of Christ, you don't just get forgiveness for your sins, you get to trade everything you are for everything He is. That means you don't just get to go to heaven someday, you get a whole new identity here on earth!

When God sees you, all He sees is the sufficiency (that's a fancy word for good-enough-ness) of His Son. Your inadequacies (or not-enough-ness) are hidden and covered by Jesus. Everything that is good and perfect about Jesus is *who you are now!*

Psalm 36:7 says, "How *priceless* is your unfailing love, O God! People take refuge in the shadow of your wings" (NIV). This verse means two very important things. Let's break it down.

First, because God's love is priceless, you are priceless! (Remember, whatever is true about Him is credited to you too.)

Second, everything that is Not-Enough about you is covered by God's Enough-ness. Your inadequacies are literally hidden behind the shadow of His greatness.

Have you ever noticed what happens to your shadow when a giant cloud gets between you and the sun? The shadow of the cloud swallows up your shadow. That's exactly what this verse means. The shadow of God's Son swallows up all of your imperfections. God only sees the perfection of His Son when He sees you.

So, the correct answer to "Who Are You Really?" is

> I am everything God knows and feels about
> His Son, Jesus. I'm *priceless!*

Chances are, whenever we are feeling like we aren't enough, we have forgotten *who we are* and *whose we are.* My hope and prayer is that God will use all the fun and crazy feelings you experience during this time of your life to remind you *who you really are* in Christ!

Together, we'll remind ourselves of who we are in Christ by fully embracing our feelings and taking them to the feet of Jesus. Every day, we'll read from the famous songbook of feelings (Psalms) and pray through what we are feeling compared to the truth of what God's Word says.

You will be tempted over the next few years to compare yourself to a lot of other things besides God's Word. You might compare yourself to friends, older siblings, the "popular" crowd, or the carefully chosen and often Photoshopped pictures you see on social media. There is one thing you need to know: comparing yourself to anything other than the truth of God's Word is risky business. Comparison is the thief of joy. I can almost guarantee you that you will constantly struggle with feeling like you are not enough if you are sizing yourself up to anyone or anything else but the truth of *who you really are* in Christ.

Join me in building a love relationship with your Heavenly Daddy, who adores you and sent His Son to make up for everything you don't think is good enough about yourself. It's as simple as reading a few verses from His Word, praying it back to Him, and then giving Him a chance to supernaturally take over your mind, heart, and soul.

Let's give it a try together.

PSALM 36:5–9 NIV

YOUR LOVE, LORD, REACHES TO THE HEAVENS,
 YOUR FAITHFULNESS TO THE SKIES.
YOUR RIGHTEOUSNESS IS LIKE THE HIGHEST MOUNTAINS,
 YOUR JUSTICE LIKE THE GREAT DEEP.
 YOU, LORD, PRESERVE BOTH PEOPLE AND ANIMALS.

Dear Faithful Father,

It's hard to understand how Your love for me could be limitless. It's as high as the heavens! Your righteousness will never run out. It's enough to cover all my imperfections. I don't have to worry about not being enough, because You are always enough for me. When I think of how big and amazing You are, I am overwhelmed.

You even take care of the animals, which
means You will surely take care of me!

HOW PRICELESS IS YOUR UNFAILING LOVE, O GOD!
PEOPLE TAKE REFUGE IN THE SHADOW OF YOUR WINGS.

Dear Jesus,

Your love is priceless! Thank You for trans-
ferring Your priceless value to me. I love
who I am in Your eyes and who I get to be
because of You. Thank You for covering all
of my imperfections in Your big shadow of
protection. It's a relief to hide behind You.

THEY FEAST ON THE ABUNDANCE OF YOUR HOUSE;
YOU GIVE THEM DRINK FROM YOUR RIVER OF DELIGHTS.
FOR WITH YOU IS THE FOUNTAIN OF LIFE;
IN YOUR LIGHT WE SEE LIGHT.

Dear Holy Spirit,

Remind me who I am in Christ. Shine light
on the truth of what God thinks about
me. Fill me with abundance when I feel like

I'm not enough. My heart is running over.
I come to You for a drink, and You are a
river! You never stop flowing and filling my
soul with delight.

If you have never traded your not-enough-ness for God's
enough-ness by accepting His gift of salvation, pray this
simple prayer asking Jesus to cover you with His love:

Jesus,

I don't think I am covered by You, and I
would like to be Yours. I know I fall short
of the perfection of heaven. I have sinned,
and I need You to forgive me. I believe You
died for me on the cross to pay for my
sins. May I please trade my sin for everything that is right about You? Come into
my life, and give me a new identity in You.
Thank You with all my heart!

Day 2

When I feel **ABANDONED** ...
I'm *wanted* by God

When the whole world walks out, your Heavenly Daddy walks in!

God will not abandon you. It is contrary to His nature. He embraces you, loves you, takes delight in you. He wants to be with you! He runs toward you singing crazy, happy, love songs because He is your proud Father. For real, that is exactly what He wrote to you in His Word (and He cannot lie): "For the LORD your God is living among you. He is a mighty savior. He will take delight in you with gladness. With his love, he will calm all your fears. He will rejoice over you with joyful songs" (Zeph. 3:17).

You were never meant to feel the pain of being abandoned. That's not what God wanted for you. When sin came into our world, one of its most terrible side effects was that God's creatures became broken, hurting people who would break and hurt other people's hearts.

Have you ever failed a test you really wanted to pass? You studied and tried your best, but you just didn't have the answers or the ability at that particular moment to pass. The same can be true of people who fail you. Sometimes they don't want to fail, but they do. Because of sin, they are broken and fall short of being who they are supposed to be for you.

People make mistakes, but God doesn't. God will not fail you. He will not leave you or forsake you—and not because He has to. He holds you close because He *wants* to. He allowed His own Son to die on the cross and pay the penalty for your sin because He wanted to be with you. He chose you!

You may feel abandoned because you don't have a friend or boyfriend or father you can trust. God is your forever companion. He is the lover of your soul, the only One who can completely satisfy the desires of your heart today and always.

Listen to His invitation and promises, and feel free to talk openly with Him.

MY HEART HAS HEARD YOU SAY, "COME AND TALK WITH ME."
AND MY HEART RESPONDS, "LORD, I AM COMING."

PSALM 27:8–13

Dear Heavenly Father,

I just want to say thank You for listening to me and for making me feel so important. Daddy, that means so much. I'm honored that You want to spend time with me. I love how You understand my deepest thoughts, even the ones I can't put into words. You are my safe haven. I can tell You everything that is happening in my life, and You don't reject me.

DO NOT TURN YOUR BACK ON ME.
DO NOT REJECT YOUR SERVANT IN ANGER.
YOU HAVE ALWAYS BEEN MY HELPER.
DON'T LEAVE ME NOW; DON'T ABANDON ME,
O GOD OF MY SALVATION!

Dear Redeemer,

I am beyond grateful that You delight in me and want to have a personal relation-ship with me. I don't want to hold anything back from You. Lord, You are my comfort, my peace, my closest friend. Even when I stray from You or run away, You pursue me and bring me back on the right path. You pick me up and carry me. Lord, I want to be so close to You that I feel Your heartbeat. Teach me Your ways so I can walk in Your truth.

EVEN IF MY FATHER AND MOTHER ABANDON ME,
    THE LORD WILL HOLD ME CLOSE.
TEACH ME HOW TO LIVE, O LORD.
    LEAD ME ALONG THE RIGHT PATH.

Lord Jesus,

Thank You that no matter what happens to me on this earth, no one can take away my relationship with You. Thank You for the promise that You will never leave me or forsake me. You will never abandon me. Come close, and help me know what to do and what to think when people disappoint me.

YET I AM CONFIDENT I WILL SEE THE LORD'S GOODNESS WHILE I AM HERE IN THE LAND OF THE LIVING.

Oh Daddy,

I just can't stop smiling. It is so cool to know that I have an everlasting companion. I don't ever have to worry about going through life alone or not having friends, because You are my best friend. I don't have to worry about having a boyfriend because You will provide godly relationships for me in Your perfect timing. I won't even have to go looking for them, because You will bring them to me. Thank You that I don't have to wait until I get to heaven to experience Your goodness. I can start to experience Your blessings right now.

Did you see the invitation in Psalm 27:8? Your Heavenly Daddy invites you to come and talk to Him. Use this space to start talking to Him today. Tell Him how you feel (write a prayer if you want to), or just ask Him your tough questions. Write down the desires of your heart, and give God a chance to come close to you. He wants to hear from you. He promises to answer you with goodness not some far-away day in heaven, but here and now, in the land of the living!

I WILL SEE THE GOODNESS OF THE LORD
IN THE LAND OF THE LIVING. (NIV)

Day 3

When I feel **AFRAID** ...
I'm *fearless* because
God is with me

Would you rather . . .

- pet a spider or a mouse?

- stand face-to-face with an angry dog or your school principal?

- speak in front of five thousand strangers or sing in front of fifty friends?

What is your biggest fear?

Here's a page from my journal two-and-a-half months before the car wreck that changed everything:

Sophomore Goals (August 2006)

1. Encourage my friends.

2. I want God to be my BEST friend, who I talk to hours each day.

3. Read my Bible before school.

4. Every day, smile and say "Hi" to ten people I don't know.

5. Stand out and be different. Show my class what a godly girl is like.

6. Lead someone to Jesus!

Lord, You know I realize I'm NOT PERFECT, and I fail You every single day. I know that when I say I want to accomplish all of these things, most likely I will not succeed. God, if I could focus on improving one thing this year, I want it to be BOLDNESS! I know that is what I need to make a difference. I have prayed continually for You to do great things with my life, but in order to follow through, I will need the boldness and courage it requires. I want my relationship with You to be evident to everyone. I want to lead many people to Christ. I want to be bold enough not to cave in to peer pressure. I want to be a bold leader who stands up for Christ. God bless this year and use me to accomplish the IMPOSSIBLE! I am open and ready to be used for Your glory!

I had some big goals going into my sophomore year of high school. There was just one problem—I was afraid to talk to people, especially about spiritual things. I did okay if I was giving a preplanned speech or presentation, but when put on the spot with a few friends, I was very shy. I wanted to be bold about my faith so badly, but I was afraid to be myself.

Less than three months after I prayed for boldness, God answered my prayer in a way I didn't expect. Because of my brain injury, I became uninhibited and didn't care what anyone thought about me. I said everything that came to my mind out loud, especially when it had to do with God. I had the goal of leading one person to Christ my sophomore year. Now, more than a decade later, thousands of people in my hometown and all over the country have come to Christ because my story shouts to others that God is real.

Don't panic! I'm not saying you have to hurt your brain in order to become fearless. You just have to let God take over your heart and mind. My story is really less about my injury and more about God answering my prayer for boldness by consuming me with His love and presence.

God wants to take away your fear and make you fearless. He will find a good way to make it happen if you ask Him to.

We tend to think courage is about us trying harder or being braver or having more faith. Really, courage is about God's love. First John 4:18 says, "There is no fear in love. But perfect love drives out fear . . . The one who fears is not made perfect in love" (NIV). The opposite of fear is not courage or faith; it's love, God's love. Conquering your fears has more to do with *who God is* than with who you are.

You can read about being fearless in Psalm 27. Underline or highlight the parts that talk about who God is. Notice especially whether there is more information about who God is or more about who you are.

THE LORD IS MY LIGHT AND MY SALVATION—
    SO WHY SHOULD I BE AFRAID?
THE LORD IS MY FORTRESS, PROTECTING ME FROM DANGER,
    SO WHY SHOULD I TREMBLE?
WHEN EVIL PEOPLE COME TO DEVOUR ME,
    WHEN MY ENEMIES AND FOES ATTACK ME,
    THEY WILL STUMBLE AND FALL.
THOUGH A MIGHTY ARMY SURROUNDS ME,
    MY HEART WILL NOT BE AFRAID.
EVEN IF I AM ATTACKED,
    I WILL REMAIN CONFIDENT.

THE ONE THING I ASK OF THE LORD—
    THE THING I SEEK MOST—
IS TO LIVE IN THE HOUSE OF THE LORD ALL THE DAYS OF MY LIFE,
    DELIGHTING IN THE LORD'S PERFECTIONS
    AND MEDITATING IN HIS TEMPLE.
FOR HE WILL CONCEAL ME THERE WHEN TROUBLES COME;
    HE WILL HIDE ME IN HIS SANCTUARY.
    HE WILL PLACE ME OUT OF REACH ON A HIGH ROCK.

Priceless

Dear Almighty Creator,

I want to be fearless! I love how in 2 Timothy 1:7 You promise that You have not given me a spirit of fear but of love, power, and a sound mind. Father, I crown You with praise. I lift up my hands and shout, "Holy, Holy, Holy are You, Lord God Almighty!"

Thank You, Daddy, that I don't have to fear because You are by my side directing me every single step of the way. Drown out my fears with Your perfect love! Help me never forget You are right beside me protecting me. I want to be Your fearless warrior.

What goals would you set for yourself this year if you were not afraid to go for them?

Write your own prayer asking God to help you be bold and fearless.

Day 4

When I feel **ALONE** . . .
I'm *surrounded* by God.

I'm thinking of a science term that begins with a *G* and ends with a *Y*. It has seven letters and three syllables. Can you guess it?

$$G \_ \_ \_ \_ \_ Y$$

Here's another hint: It's the reason you aren't floating in the air right now. It's the reason your pen will fall to the ground if you drop it. Go ahead, try it: hold your pen out, and let go.

Congratulations!!! I knew you'd guess "gravity" after your pen fell to the floor!

Now try walking to another place (any place you choose) without taking gravity with you. Not possible, you say?

Think about it carefully. Is there any place you can go and escape gravity?

Did *outer space* come to mind? Nope! Even in outer space, a small amount of gravity known as microgravity is still at work. It's what keeps the moon in orbit around the earth and the earth in orbit around the sun. Even in galaxies that are light-years away, gravity is still present.

The same is true about God. He is everywhere always. Which means that wherever you go, God goes before you and behind you and above you and beneath you. You are completely surrounded by your Heavenly Father at all times! It is impossible for you to be apart from Him, which also means that *you are never alone.*

YOU GO BEFORE ME AND FOLLOW ME.
    YOU PLACE YOUR HAND OF BLESSING ON MY HEAD.
SUCH KNOWLEDGE IS TOO WONDERFUL FOR ME,
    TOO GREAT FOR ME TO UNDERSTAND!

I CAN NEVER ESCAPE FROM YOUR SPIRIT!
    I CAN NEVER GET AWAY FROM YOUR PRESENCE!
IF I GO UP TO HEAVEN, YOU ARE THERE;
    IF I GO DOWN TO THE GRAVE YOU ARE THERE.

PSALM 139:5–10

IF I RIDE THE WINGS OF THE MORNING,
      IF I DWELL BY THE FARTHEST OCEANS,
EVEN THERE YOUR HAND WILL GUIDE ME,
      AND YOUR STRENGTH WILL SUPPORT ME.

There you have it: absolute proof that you cannot be alone—ever! I know, sweet girl, I know what you're thinking. It *is* possible to *feel* alone. I've felt it too. But just because you feel something doesn't make it true. Feelings are often warning signals reminding us to cry out to God. Feeling lonely might be the very thing God uses to remind you that you are never alone.

Try praying this prayer next time you feel alone:

> Dear Heavenly Daddy,
>
> Reach down from heaven today and remind me that You are right beside me. Please cradle me in Your everlasting arms and whisper hope in my ear. It's so comforting to know I don't have to go through one moment by myself. Thank You that I don't have to fear even when I walk into new situations, take a test, or stay at home by myself. I never have to worry because You are holding me on every side.

I'm secure because You promise to be my lifelong companion. I can never fall away from Your presence. I run to You today with all of who I am (and all of who I'm not). It's an honor to be Yours forever.

You can ask to feel God's presence every minute of every day. Ask God to reach down from heaven and give you a big hug. Ask God to hold you in His arms when you can't go to sleep. Ask God to do something to show you how much He loves you.

God knows what will make you feel special. He cares about what is important to you. It could be numbers or color, bringing a Bible verse to your mind, showing you a beautiful rainbow or sunset. He knows exactly how to get your attention in a way that you will know it has to be Him reaching out to remind You that He is always with you. You are never alone!

Circle the places you feel most alone:

School	**Home**
Church	**Lunch**
In Bed at Night	**Weekends**
After-School Activities	**Math Class**

Other: _____

Priceless

ACTION PLAN

1. Ask God to prove He is with you in those places.

2. Look for someone else who might feel alone there too and encourage him or her.

3. Take a phone break for twenty-four hours and tell someone face-to-face that you feel lonely. Watch what God does.

Day 5

When I feel **ANGRY** ...
I'm *trusting* God to defend me

Name something or someone that makes you angry:

Now try something crazy: Go stand in front of a mirror and explain to yourself OUT LOUD why that thing or person makes you angry. Get sassy with it! Get it all out! Come on, try it. I know you have a mirror somewhere nearby.

What did your face look like in the mirror while you talked about your anger issues? Did you scare yourself, or did you start laughing? Put an *X* on the scale below to rate how you looked:

SCARY ———————————— SILLY

Did it feel good to get some of that anger out? Have you ever been angry at God? If so, have you ever told Him why you are angry at Him?

God already knows your thoughts so you might as well say it like it is. You have permission to be 100 percent real with God. Let all your anger out, and tell Him everything. Tell God about the injustice or what someone did to you and how much it hurt. Get the pain out loud. You can even tell God that you're angry at Him. Maybe He didn't answer your prayers the way you wanted Him to. Maybe He disappointed you.

Try telling God why you are angry. Take a few minutes to write about it here:

The more I talk to God, the more He changes the desires of my heart to want what He wants. God sees the big picture. He knows what is best for me. The more I talk to Him about how I feel, the easier it is to trust Him to take care of my problems. After all, He is much better at solving my problems than I am.

Who would you rather have defending your cause, you (the girl who looks crazy when you yell in the mirror) or God (the One who owns and controls everything in the universe)? When I get angry, I just picture God holding the whole universe in the palm of His hand, and it makes me feel calm and peaceful.

It might make you feel better to know that God gets angry too. He understands. The feeling of anger isn't a sin; it's what we do with our anger that can become a sin. We have to take our anger to the truth of God's Word *before* we let it loose to affect our actions.

Here's a random question: Have you ever tried to put toothpaste back into the tube after you squeezed it out? Newsflash: It can't be done. Once it's out there, it's out there. The same is true with our words, especially our angry words.

Anger becomes a sin when I lose my temper, become bitter in my heart, or lash out to hurt someone. However, anger can be a good thing if it moves me to action. It's important to have anger against injustice and sin. Anger can make us passionate about defending the helpless and protecting our freedoms.

Here's my best advice about what to do when you feel angry:

1. *Don't speak or act right away.*

2. *Pray first. Ask God to defend your cause, and let Him fight for you first before you fight for yourself. He might just solve your problem better than you could.*

3. *Ask God to turn your anger into passion for a good cause. Channel your passion into a purpose.*

It's your turn to try it. Try praying these words *out loud*:

Dear Faithful Fighting Father,

The feeling of anger is so real. I want to break free from those chains today. I want to have the opposite of anger, which is love, joy, and peace. I want to be controlled by Your Spirit, who lives inside of me, instead of being controlled by my wounded heart. Please don't allow anger to control me

today. I choose to be filled with Your
peace that passes all understanding. Help
me see the people who make me angry
the way You see them. Change my heart to
desire what You desire!

TAKE DELIGHT IN THE LORD,
    AND HE WILL GIVE YOU YOUR HEART'S DESIRES.

COMMIT EVERYTHING YOU DO TO THE LORD.
    TRUST HIM, AND HE WILL HELP YOU.
HE WILL MAKE YOUR INNOCENCE RADIATE LIKE THE DAWN,
    AND THE JUSTICE OF YOUR CAUSE WILL SHINE LIKE
        THE NOONDAY SUN.

BE STILL IN THE PRESENCE OF THE LORD,
    AND WAIT PATIENTLY FOR HIM TO ACT.

PSALM 37:4-9

Lord Jesus,

Today I want to pray for help. Help me
love my enemies. Help me love the person
who lied to me. Help me love the person

who disappointed me. Lord, I could go on
and on. Thank You for showing us how we
can love our enemies. On the cross, You
prayed, "Father, forgive them for they
do not know what they are doing." You
died on the cross and shed Your blood
so I could be free from the feelings of
bitterness that consume me. Today, I
choose to let go of my anger. I choose
to trust You to defend my cause or turn
it into something good!

DON'T WORRY ABOUT EVIL PEOPLE WHO PROSPER
    OR FRET ABOUT THEIR WICKED SCHEMES.

STOP BEING ANGRY!
    TURN FROM YOUR RAGE!
DO NOT LOSE YOUR TEMPER—
    IT ONLY LEADS TO HARM.
FOR THE WICKED WILL BE DESTROYED,
    BUT THOSE WHO TRUST IN THE LORD WILL POSSESS
        THE LAND.

Your anger over injustice could turn into a dream to change the world! How could you turn your anger into a positive action. For example, you might pray for the person who hurt you, fight for a cause, feed the homeless, raise money for cancer, be a friend to a disabled student, or something like that.

What is God saying to your heart today? Can you think of a good cause to get angry about?

Day 6

When I feel **ANNOYED** ...
I'm *free* to choose thoughts that please God

Next to each of the following people, write down the percentage of time that they annoy you whenever you are together.

For example: **Little Brother:** _75%_

Brother: _____ **Parents:** _____

Favorite Teacher: _____ **Sister:** _____

Coach: _____ **Least Favorite Teacher:** _____

Best Friend: _____ **Clingy Friend:** _____

Boyfriend: _____

Other Annoying People in Your Life: _____

Take a good look at those percentages, because that is the amount of time that you are allowing others to control you. That is the percentage of time you are trapped in bondage to your feelings when you could be living free.

Whenever you feel annoyed, you are giving someone else power over you. You are choosing to put your preferences first instead of putting others first. I call that the "Me-Trap." When life is all about "me," you are guaranteed to feel annoyed most of the day.

I know all about the Me-Trap. Because of my brain injury, I am very easily annoyed by loud noises. My little brother always had to be quiet around the house. He even hid in the pantry to eat potato chips because the sound of his crunching drove me crazy. Everyone catered to me because I was injured, until eventually I realized there was a better way. Even with my injury, I could still choose to control my attitude. I noticed I was starting to tolerate loud noises as long as it was something I was interested in, but when it came to things that only my brother enjoyed (like sports on TV), I got annoyed.

Being annoyed is an attitude of the heart. I get annoyed when I am consumed with selfish thoughts. Often, I get annoyed by things I can't control, like how loud my brother chews or how loud my little cousins scream. I can, however, control my attitude. I can ask God to give me joy and patience. I can choose to remove myself and go spend time somewhere quiet. I can wear earplugs, or better yet, I can choose to focus on others. Whenever it comes to living a life pleasing to God, we always have options. We are free to follow Him. We don't have to live in bondage to our feelings or the things that easily annoy us.

The immediate cure for being annoyed is tapping into the fruit of the Spirit, which includes love, joy, peace, patience, gentleness, and self-control (Gal. 5). None of these qualities come from me; they come from God. When I choose to be controlled by the Spirit rather than by my selfish desires, I am free to put up with the things that usually annoy me.

The long-term cure for being annoyed is helping others. When I am focused on others, I am not focused on myself. The more I am focused on pleasing God and living for Him, the less I fall into the Me-Trap of getting annoyed by every little thing.

Choose to face the day with a smile. Before you even get out of bed, say out loud, "Today is going to be a GREAT day! I am free to control my attitude. I am free to help others. I am free to live a life pleasing to God!"

HOW CAN I KNOW ALL THE SINS LURKING IN MY HEART?
CLEANSE ME FROM THESE HIDDEN FAULTS.

Dear Wise Counselor,

Please bring to light any sin hidden in my
heart and mind. Satan controls whatever
I keep hidden, but You, Jesus, heal whatever I
bring into the light. You are the Light of the
world. Cleanse me of my selfish thoughts.
Create a clean heart in me. I want to be
controlled by You, the Living Hope.

KEEP YOUR SERVANT FROM DELIBERATE SINS!
    DON'T LET THEM CONTROL ME.
THEN I WILL BE FREE OF GUILT
    AND INNOCENT OF GREAT SIN.

Dear Heavenly Father,

I don't want to be controlled by negativity.
Help me break free from the Me-Trap. I
choose to be controlled by the Spirit, who
is alive inside of me. I don't worship a God
who is dead. I worship a God who is alive
and powerful. Reveal to me those things

that I am allowing to control me. I don't want anything to have power over me except Your Word.

MAY THE WORDS OF MY MOUTH
    AND THE MEDITATION OF MY HEART
BE PLEASING TO YOU,
    O LORD, MY ROCK AND MY REDEEMER.

Daddy,

I remember the Scripture that describes how our mouths say the things that fill our hearts (Matt. 12:34–35). Help me store up good things in my heart, so that when I speak, good will come out. I want to replace all those annoying feelings that I have for my parents, my teachers, and my friends with feelings of grace and patience. All I have to do is stop and ask You for help. Thank You for being my Rock and my Redeemer!

Try starting every day this week on your knees praying for the people who annoy you most. Ask God to give you patience and options when you have to deal with annoying situations or people. Ask God to set you free from the Me-Trap.

Write a prayer here for the person who scored the most percentage points on the annoying chart today:

Day 7

When I feel **ASHAMED** . . .
I'm *forgiven*

I'm about to ask you to do something crazy. Are you up for it? Please follow these instructions very carefully.

1. *Put your pillow in front of your face.*

2. *Take a selfie. Come on, do it!*

3. *Now put the pillow down so you can look at the selfie.*

What do you see in your pillow selfie? Do you see the imperfections in your hair, your face, or makeup?

No, of course not! YOU SEE YOUR PILLOW!

Do you know that when God looks at you, He does not see any of your imperfections? He sees His Son—period. If you've asked Jesus to forgive your sins and believe what He did on the cross counted for you, you are completely covered in His righteousness. God doesn't see any flaws in you anymore. He only sees all the goodness and perfection of His Son. You have nothing to be ashamed of. It's like covering your bad hair day or acne flare-up with your pillowcase. You look fabulous to Him!

Let me explain. Yes, God is grieved by your sin. And yes, there are consequences when you make poor choices. But when you confess your sin, God forgives you and cleanses you through the shed blood of His Son, Jesus. You get to exchange your sin and shame for the righteousness of Jesus. There is a big difference between guilt and shame. Guilt is feeling bad about something you have done; shame is feeling bad about who you are. Your worth and value lie in *who* you are *in Christ.* You are a priceless daughter of the King. God never intended you to carry around shame.

BLESSED IS THE ONE
   WHOSE TRANSGRESSIONS ARE FORGIVEN,
   WHOSE SINS ARE COVERED.
BLESSED IS THE ONE
   WHOSE SIN THE LORD DOES NOT COUNT AGAINST THEM

PSALM 32:1–7 NIV

. . . .

WHEN I KEPT SILENT,
    MY BONES WASTED AWAY

. . . .

FOR DAY AND NIGHT
    YOUR HAND WAS HEAVY ON ME;
MY STRENGTH WAS SAPPED
    AS IN THE HEAT OF SUMMER.

THEN I ACKNOWLEDGED MY SIN TO YOU
    AND DID NOT COVER UP MY INIQUITY.
I SAID, "I WILL CONFESS
    MY TRANSGRESSIONS TO THE LORD."
AND YOU FORGAVE
    THE GUILT OF MY SIN.

. . . .

YOU ARE MY HIDING PLACE;
    YOU WILL PROTECT ME FROM TROUBLE
    AND SURROUND ME WITH SONGS OF DELIVERANCE.

Lord Jesus,

I just want to take a moment to reflect on You and how cool You are. To think that You died on the cross and paid the full penalty for my sin! You covered my shame! You covered my regrets! You covered it ALL on Calvary! I can find complete forgiveness and freedom in You. The great exchange is my sin for Your righteousness. I am covered by the blood of the Lamb. Thank You for clothing me in Your spotless white robe of perfection. I don't deserve it, but I receive it. It is such an honor to call Your righteousness my own!

Father God,

I know that shame is not from You. It is the fingerprint of Satan. I want to be clothed in something better, something honorable, something praiseworthy. As I go through my day, help me refuse to take on the garment of shame. I look to You to find my strength and security this day. Shame is feeling bad about who I am. Lord, I could never feel bad about who I am because I am a daughter of the King of kings. I am Your daughter. You claim me and chose me as Your own. Today, I celebrate who I am in You.

Oh Daddy, thank You! Just thank You! It is so awesome to be forgiven by You and to experience that freedom. It is like a fresh start. I can get back on track and head in the right direction. Help me fix my eyes on You. Teach me which way to go.

Holy Spirit,

Please bring to the light any bad thoughts or actions that I need to confess. Satan controls what is in the darkness. But Lord, You can heal whatever I bring into the light. God, thank You for the promise that You will forgive me and cleanse me when I confess my sins. You will wash me whiter than snow.

Do you have anything you need to confess to God? Is there anything that you've done or forgotten to do that makes you feel ashamed? God's Word says that whatever we uncover by admitting we are sorry, God covers—for good, forever!

Write it on a napkin (the thing that you are ashamed of). Ask God to forgive you for it. Then go flush it down the toilet! If God has forgiven it, then it's time for you to get rid of it! Stop condemning yourself. Stop carrying your shame around. Flush it!

When I feel **AWKWARD** ...
I'm *confident* in God's love for me

Would you be willing to take the Weirdo Test for me? This test is proven to decide once and for all if you are, in fact, a weirdo. Wouldn't you like to know? All you have to do is answer these simple questions. Just circle the first answer that comes to your mind. Don't be nervous. Ready?

I. When you eat french fries, do you ...

a) squirt ketchup all over them?

b) keep ketchup on the side for dipping?

2. When you eat spaghetti, do you . . .

a) cut it up into pieces?

b) twirl it onto your fork?

3. When you eat Oreos, do you . . .

a) twist them in half and lick the cream?

b) throw the whole cookie into your mouth?

Okay, now for the results. Drumroll, please! Guess what?

You are not a weirdo.

No matter what you answered, no matter how you eat your french fries, spaghetti, and Oreos, no matter what you do, you are not a weirdo! You are made in the image of God. God is not a weirdo; He is wonderful, so you are too! Besides, at least half of the people in America have the same weird eating habits that you do, so you aren't weird; you are perfectly normal!

Your body might be in the middle of a lot of changes that make you feel a little awkward at times. You are transitioning physically, emotionally, and spiritually all at once, which is a lot to deal with. You are moving from being dependent on parents and teachers to discovering your own independence. You are learning how to hear God's voice for yourself for the first time. It's all very new and exciting and, at times, totally overwhelming.

What do you do when you trip down the stairs at school because you are suddenly three inches taller and two shoe sizes bigger than you were last month?

What do you do when your face breaks out in pimples on picture day?

What do you do when you start your period at school and you weren't prepared?

You do what Psalm 57 says: cry out to the Lord.

I CRY OUT TO GOD MOST HIGH,

TO GOD WHO WILL FULFILL HIS PURPOSE FOR ME.

HE WILL SEND HELP FROM HEAVEN TO RESCUE ME.

PSALM 57:2-10

When you feel awkward or uncertain, cry out to God. He will help you. He will fulfill His purpose for you. No terrifying experience can mess up His plans for you! The Most High God is on your side and is able to deploy all the powers of heaven to rescue you at any given moment. Stick with Him!

MY HEART IS CONFIDENT IN YOU, O GOD;

   MY HEART IS CONFIDENT.

   NO WONDER I CAN SING YOUR PRAISES!

Recognize that while your world is constantly changing, your confidence can only come from God, who never changes. He is the one certain, secure thing right now. Friends will come and go. Boyfriends will come and go. Fashion will come and go. Popularity will come and go. God is your only constant. Sing His praises!

WAKE UP, MY HEART!

   WAKE UP, O LYRE AND HARP!

   I WILL WAKE THE DAWN WITH MY SONG.

I WILL THANK YOU, LORD, AMONG ALL THE PEOPLE.

   I WILL SING YOUR PRAISES AMONG THE NATIONS.

Put your focus on God and not yourself. When you are thinking about you, chances are you will feel awkward. How could you not? Everything is new. Here's a helpful tip: no one else is thinking about you as much as you are thinking about you, except God. He is the only one who thinks about you *more* than you think about you. Try thinking about Him more than you think about you.

FOR YOUR UNFAILING LOVE IS AS HIGH AS THE HEAVENS. YOUR FAITHFULNESS REACHES TO THE CLOUDS.

No matter what happens over the next years, one thing is certain: God loves you. His love will never fail you. It is higher than your growth spurt, bigger than your embarrassing moments, and deeper than the hole you want to crawl into when you feel awkward.

This time of transition in your life is difficult, yes. Awkward at times, too! But it is also a season that God perfectly designed so He could show up and be your hero! He longs to come to your rescue. He longs to be your confidence. He loves to be your everything!

Father,

Today I want to turn my awkward feelings into joy! I know You love me just as I am. Please turn my anxious thoughts into confidence. I know You didn't create me to blend in and be like everyone else. You made me unique, and I want to celebrate that fact. There is no one exactly like me in the whole wide world—no one with the same fingerprint or the same DNA, no one who has a brain like mine. Wow!

That gives me chills! Feeling awkward is really the same as being insecure. I choose to view myself the way You view me. I am chosen. I am one-of-a-kind. Father, You crafted me in Your image. That is such an honor. No one else has my story. I am a precious jewel. I am Yours. Today I give all my awkwardness to You. I choose instead to seek after You as if I am seeking for a hidden treasure. You are my security and my stronghold.

On any given day, at least half the people in your world are feeling just as awkward as you are (with the eating habits from the Weirdo Test and other strange habits, too). So here's a challenge: Look for someone else to rescue today. Find someone sitting alone, someone who had a bad day, or someone else who is hurting. Tell that person about God's love and great and personal plans for him or her.

Day 9

When I feel **BEAUTIFUL** ...
I'm *reflecting* God's glory

What is your favorite photo of yourself? What do you love about it?

What makes you feel beautiful? Why?

Do you feel prettier when you are decked out fancy head to toe or when you are all-natural and comfy with your hair in a messy bun?

What do you think is the most beautiful feature God designed for you?

What part of you (either inside or out) best reflects God's beauty? (your eyes, your smile, your hair, your heart, your sense of humor, your songs, etc.)

If you are having trouble answering any of these questions, read and pray through the verses of Psalm 45, then come back and try to answer them again.

YOU LOVE JUSTICE AND HATE EVIL.
THEREFORE GOD, YOUR GOD, HAS ANOINTED YOU,
POURING OUT THE OIL OF JOY ON YOU MORE THAN
ON ANYONE ELSE.
MYRRH, ALOES, AND CASSIA PERFUME YOUR ROBES.
IN IVORY PALACES THE MUSIC OF STRINGS
ENTERTAINS YOU.
KINGS' DAUGHTERS ARE AMONG YOUR NOBLE WOMEN.
AT YOUR RIGHT SIDE STANDS THE QUEEN,
WEARING JEWELRY OF FINEST GOLD FROM OPHIR!

PSALM 45:7–11

Dear Creator,

Thank You that I can feel beautiful because
You are beautiful in me. You have anointed
me with Your joy. It may be through a
smile, laughter, or encouragement. Father,
my prayer is that I would carry a hint of
Your glory. I want to be the sunshine in
someone else's day! Lord, allow me to help
someone else feel important, valued, or
loved. Lord, help me find my inner beauty
today. I'm so excited because I know that

inner beauty comes from when I spend more time with You through prayer and reading Your Word. May I never take for granted that the Bible is Your love letter to me. I want to be a better reflection of You. Help me shine Your love and kindness to the world.

LISTEN TO ME, O ROYAL DAUGHTER; TAKE TO HEART WHAT I SAY. FORGET YOUR PEOPLE. . . .

Wow! Lord, I just have to smile. Thank You for choosing me. You picked me out of a crowd and said, "I want her." It's beyond my comprehension that You know my name and love me. Even greater yet, You have a huge plan for me. It's overwhelming. I am shouting out loud, "I am Your daughter. I am a child of the King of kings. It is such an honor to be Yours, Daddy."

FOR YOUR ROYAL HUSBAND DELIGHTS IN YOUR BEAUTY; HONOR HIM, FOR HE IS YOUR LORD.

Thank You for the promise that You "delight" in me and that You are my "royal husband." Wow! It's hard to comprehend that I have a wedding in my future in heaven one day because the church is the bride of Christ, and I am part of the church because I have accepted You as my Lord and Savior. No matter what happens on this earth, I have a future in heaven with You for all of eternity with no tears and no suffering. Someday I will get to heaven and get to see You face-to-face, which as You know is "the dream." But until that day, I pray that on this earth I can be sold out for You 110 percent and can be controlled by the Spirit and by the truth of Your Word. I want to be a living reflection of You, Jesus! Now that is BEAUTIFUL!

How does it feel to know that God "delights in your beauty" (v. 11)?

Write your own prayer in response to Him choosing you to reflect a part of His glory that no one else can:

True beauty is reflected in the eyes. Whenever people you know begin to make poor choices, you can see it in their eyes. They don't have innocent eyes anymore. That's why some people are less attractive the more you get to know them, and some people get more attractive as their inner beauty comes out. God promises to "pour out the oil of joy on you more than on anyone else" (Ps. 45:7). When you are close to Him, He enhances your inner and outer beauty.

When you are spending time with Jesus, it is reflected in your eyes and in your smile. You shine and radiate the love of Jesus. Your eyes are a window to your soul. A girl can be physically beautiful, but if she isn't obeying God's Word (if she is doing things that harm her body and her soul) it shows in the hardness of her face and sadness of her eyes. That darkness diminishes her beauty.

Matthew 6:22–23 explains this phenomenon: "The eye is the lamp of the body. If your eyes are healthy, your whole body will be full of light. But if your eyes are unhealthy, your whole body will be full of darkness" (NIV).

If you haven't been feeling beautiful lately, ask God to shine through you again. Think about what you have been spending time looking at and putting into your soul. Fix your eyes on Jesus, the author and perfecter of your true beauty.

Consider taking this action step: invite some friends over for a Beauty Makeover Party. After you do each other's hair and makeup and take silly pictures, sit in a circle and tell each friend what you think is most beautiful about her on the inside and the outside.

Day 10

When I feel **BETRAYED** ...
I'm *giving* my burdens to God

There is something you will learn about people sooner or later; maybe you've already experienced it. Save it in your notes and remember this truth: hurting people hurt others. If you've had a friend turn on you, stab you in the back, or say cruel things to you, chances are your friend is hurting, too—and maybe even more than you. Maybe her home life is not as secure as yours, maybe she feels abandoned by another friend or parent, or maybe she's feeling insecure or threatened. Whatever the hurt is, you can't fix it; only God can. The longer wounded people carry their hurt around, the more bitter and toxic they become and the more likely they will be to hurt others.

The same goes for you. The longer you carry around the pain of betrayal, the more likely you are to start hurting others. You have to give that burden away to God as quickly as you can. The psalms tell us exactly what to do when we feel hurt or betrayed: "Give your burdens to the Lord, and He will take care of you" (Ps. 55:22). Run straight to God when your heart is hurting. Let Him heal you, and pray for Him to heal your offender too.

King David, who wrote Psalm 55, was no stranger to betrayal. His own father-in-law (Saul) tried to kill him; his son (Absalom) tried to steal his throne; and his closest friend and advisor (Ahithophel) betrayed him and devised a plot to kill him.

Most scholars think David wrote Psalm 55 about Ahithophel's betrayal. There is something you should know about this guy: Ahithophel was the grandfather of Bathsheba (2 Sam. 11:3; 23:34). Do you recognize that name? Bathsheba is the woman King David dishonored by stealing her from her husband and arranging for him to die in battle. It is very possible Ahithophel carried that shame and hurt around until the perfect opportunity presented itself for him to get even with David. The tragic ending is that Ahithophel did not succeed in hurting David; he only hurt himself. God protected David, and Ahithophel ended up so overwhelmed by his pain that he took his own life.

Hurting people hurt others, but they hurt themselves more. You don't have to worry about getting even with the people who hurt you. In the end, they will hurt themselves more than you. Give that burden to Jesus as quickly as you can so you don't fall into the same trap. Trust Him to take care of it for you. Jesus was betrayed and un-followed by His closest friends. He knows how to carry that burden for you!

PSALM 55:12–22

IT IS NOT AN ENEMY WHO TAUNTS ME—
 I COULD BEAR THAT.
IT IS NOT MY FOES WHO SO ARROGANTLY INSULT ME—
 I COULD HAVE HIDDEN FROM THEM.
INSTEAD, IT IS YOU—MY EQUAL,
 MY COMPANION AND CLOSE FRIEND.

Dear All-Powerful One,

Betrayal by a friend I trusted is a big thing. It makes me feel abandoned. It makes me feel like I'm not important, valued, or honored. But You, Father, speak the opposite. You tell me I am valued; I am important; I am worth it. You went to the cross and died so You could rescue me

and redeem me. Whenever I feel betrayed,
I run to You! Father, please cradle me in
Your arms. Hold me tight. Lord, You know
that life is hard. You understand. You were
betrayed and deserted by Your friends
when You died on the cross for me. Heal
my wounded heart like only You can.

BUT I WILL CALL ON GOD,
    AND THE LORD WILL RESCUE ME.
MORNING, NOON, AND NIGHT
    I CRY OUT IN MY DISTRESS,
    AND THE LORD HEARS MY VOICE.
HE RANSOMS ME AND KEEPS ME SAFE
    FROM THE BATTLE WAGED AGAINST ME,
    THOUGH MANY STILL OPPOSE ME.
GOD, WHO HAS RULED FOREVER,
    WILL HEAR ME AND HUMBLE THEM.

Dear Faithful One,

I'm so thankful that I can run to You,
my Best Friend. You are the only One
who will never disappoint me. I put all

my expectations in You, Jesus. This whole time I have been trying to get my friends' approval when I already had Your approval. God, today, I choose to see myself the way You see me—as important and priceless! I love how prayer is a two-way conversation when I can transfer my burdens to You and then listen to You whisper hope and healing back to my heart.

AS FOR MY COMPANION, HE BETRAYED HIS FRIENDS;
    HE BROKE HIS PROMISES.
HIS WORDS ARE AS SMOOTH AS BUTTER,
    BUT IN HIS HEART IS WAR.
HIS WORDS ARE AS SOOTHING AS LOTION,
    BUT UNDERNEATH ARE DAGGERS!

Lord,

I have felt this way—as if my friend's words were "smooth as butter" to my face, and yet "war was in her heart" because she gossiped behind my back. I give that pain to You. I pray for my enemies to know and experience Your healing too. Father, forgive them. They probably don't know how bad they are hurting me because they are hurting too.

GIVE YOUR BURDENS TO THE LORD,
AND HE WILL TAKE CARE OF YOU.
HE WILL NOT PERMIT THE GODLY TO SLIP AND FALL.

Daddy,

I just want to crawl up in Your arms today. Thank You for being my secure foundation. Please Lord, may Your loving presence comfort me and nurture my soul. I want to hear Your voice of truth. Please give me Your wisdom and insight into this situation that makes me feel betrayed. Help me see what is under the surface in my friend's life. I don't want to lash out and hurt back. It's an endless cycle. Daddy, help me love my friend with Your love. Help me move past the pain and love my friend because my friend matters to You.

Try this action step: write a love letter of forgiveness to the person who has hurt or betrayed you. Don't send it or even write it expecting to change that person. This letter is for your heart, to change your heart toward the friend who's caused you pain.

Do you feel any better now? If not, take a minute to think about what this verse says about God: "For God is not the author of confusion, but of peace" (1 Cor. 14:33 NKJV). Next, try the Peace Test to help you when decision making gets confusing. Here's how it works. First you take one of your options off the table. For example, if you are trying to decide whether or not to go to a movie with friends, pretend that you have decided NOT to go to the movie. Take that option away in your mind. How do you feel? Do you feel at peace about it? Or do you feel you are missing a great opportunity?

God gives peace not confusion. The Peace Test helps you determine if something is God's best choice or not. If you don't feel a peace about it, it's not God's choice. If you do feel more at peace when you take that option off the table, chances are God is confirming your decision. God uses His peace to guide us. Sometimes you may have to sleep on it for a night, but God will often confirm your choices with His peace or lack of it.

Do you feel better now? If not, try talking with someone you trust and respect about the things that are confusing you (a teacher, a parent, a friend, an older sibling, a youth leader at church).

HERE'S A TRUSTED ACTION PLAN
YOU CAN USE WHEN YOU FEEL CONFUSED:

1. *Go to God about it.*

2. *Go to God's Word about it.*

3. *Try the Peace Test.*

4. *Try talking to someone wiser than you.*

If these four actions line up in agreement, then be confident with your decision, and go for it! If one of these four things is conflicting with another, then go back to number one and start over at the beginning, or wait. God might not be saying "no" forever; He might just be saying "not now."

Remember, He wants you to know what to do even more than you want you to know what to do!

God says, "My sheep hear My voice, and I know them, and they follow Me" (John 10:27 NKJV). It's more about God knowing you than you knowing what is right to do. God knows how to get your attention. He will get you where He wants you to go. Even if you make the wrong choice, He is big enough and powerful enough to get you back on track.

Dear Faithful Shepherd,

Thank You for guiding me and being with me on the mountaintops as well as in the valleys. I don't want to miss even one plan You have for me today. Help me talk to You all through my day. I know You are my Companion, and You are holding my hand. Thank You for constantly directing my footsteps. I want to be so close to You that I feel Your heartbeat. Give me the courage to go where You lead. I'm clinging to You. You are my Heavenly Daddy, who holds my hand so even when I stumble and make a mistake, I can't fall flat on my face because You catch me. Help me not to give the feeling of confusion any power or authority in my life. I want to tap into Your authority. You are the author of peace and truth. There is no confusion in You. May Your voice be the loudest voice I hear and the only voice I listen to. May Your voice be the one that drives my heart today and every day.

God delights in every detail of your life. There is no problem too big or too small that you can't bring to God for help. He uses every detail of your life to write an amazing story!

Day 12

When I feel **DISAPPOINTED** ...
I'm *expecting* God to make a new path

God may have to shut a few doors in your face to get you on the new path He is carving out for you. At first when those doors shut, it can feel as if God has forgotten you. One of the things I love most about the songs in Psalms is that they are so vulnerable and honest. They give us permission to be real with God and tell Him exactly how we feel no matter how raw it sounds. Check out what the disappointed psalmist says to God in Psalm 77.

HAS THE LORD REJECTED ME FOREVER?

WILL HE NEVER AGAIN BE KIND TO ME?

IS HIS UNFAILING LOVE GONE FOREVER?

HAVE HIS PROMISES PERMANENTLY FAILED?

PSALM 77:7-19

HAS GOD FORGOTTEN TO BE GRACIOUS?

HAS HE SLAMMED THE DOOR ON HIS COMPASSION?

It sure sounds like this psalm writer was having a no-good, very-bad day. But once he was honest with God and expressed his true feelings, he had room in his heart and his mind to remember the good things God had done for him in the past. Aren't you glad we can be honest and tell God how we really feel? After all, He is the one who gave us those feelings as a gift. Keep reading.

BUT THEN I RECALL ALL YOU HAVE DONE, O LORD;

I REMEMBER YOUR WONDERFUL DEEDS OF LONG AGO.

THEY ARE CONSTANTLY IN MY THOUGHTS.

I CANNOT STOP THINKING ABOUT YOUR MIGHTY WORKS.

O GOD, YOUR WAYS ARE HOLY.

IS THERE ANY GOD AS MIGHTY AS YOU?

YOU ARE THE GOD OF GREAT WONDERS!

YOU DEMONSTRATE YOUR AWESOME POWER AMONG

THE NATIONS.

BY YOUR STRONG ARM, YOU REDEEMED YOUR PEOPLE

. . . .

YOUR ROAD LED THROUGH THE SEA,

YOUR PATHWAY THROUGH THE MIGHTY WATERS— A PATHWAY NO ONE KNEW WAS THERE!

Why don't you try writing your own psalm to God using the pattern from Psalm 77? Start out by telling God exactly how you feel. Ask your difficult questions. Tell Him what is disappointing you today:

Now that you've got those feelings out, try listing some good things God has done for you in the past. When has He helped you or given you something you needed? If you have trouble thinking of good things, start with the air you are breathing or that the sun came up this morning.

Sometimes my greatest disappointment is *me*. Maybe you can relate. Right now you might feel so many pressures to achieve bigger and better things, to fit in, to look beautiful. You need to know that even though you may feel disappointed in yourself or think others are disappointed with you, God accepts you just as you are. He delights in you and loves you unconditionally. God loves you if you stay in bed all day or fail a test or don't make homecoming queen or don't make the sports team. You don't have to be perfect. That's one of Satan's lies. Only God is perfect. His love for you is unconditional no matter what you say or do or look like.

His timing is also perfect. Sometimes, it doesn't feel that way. Waiting is hard because it's . . . waiting. It doesn't feel great to wait. While you are waiting for Him to make a new path for you, try focusing on everything He has already done for you.

> If you are searching for a companion,
> He IS your companion.
>
> If you are searching for love,
> He IS love.
>
> If you are searching for identity,
> He IS your identity.

If you are searching for something special,
He IS your something special.

When my confidence is in God, I can never be disappointed! God has already given us all the things we are searching for! We limit our abilities when we don't embrace all that God has already given us.

I get so excited not knowing the plans for the day because it is God's story! All my expectations are in Him. God always *exceeds* my expectations and does beyond what I could hope or imagine. That's why I choose Joy; I choose Life; I choose Sunshine; I choose to Speak Positively.

Why don't you try choosing Joy with me?

Dear Faithful One,

Thank You that when I feel disappointed, I can trust in Your grace. I can grab onto the hem of Your garment and go where You lead because I know that's where miracles happen. You don't promise to answer my prayer requests according to my plans, but according to Your greater plan that will bring glory to Your name. Please show me today how to take one step forward with You and trust in You with all my heart. I have seen the work

of Your hands in the past. I'm not afraid
to trust You because I know that when
I do, the impossible is made possible! I
don't have to worry because You hold my
future. You are writing my story. Thank
You that I can trust You to get me to the
promised land in my life. I believe the best
is yet to come!

Day 13

When I feel **DUMB** . . .
I'm *wise* in God's eyes

If you could wave a magic wand and make it Opposite Day, which opposite would be the most fun for you:

- Bad food being healthy and healthy food being bad?

- Netflix benefitting your brain and homework being a waste of time?

- Short people being tall and tall people being short?

- Good grades turning into bad grades and bad grades turning into good?

What opposite would be a dream-come-true for you? It might surprise you that you don't need a magic wand to live in an opposite world. Every day with God is Opposite Day. Much of the way God works is the exact reverse of the way humans think.

For example, with God,

- It's more fun to give than to receive (Acts 20:35).

- The weakest are strongest (2 Cor. 12:9).

- You have to lose your life to save it (Matt. 16:25).

- The last will be first, and the first will be last (Matt. 20:16).

Who or what makes you feel dumb?

If you have ever felt dumb before, you might like these verses:

"I will destroy the wisdom of the wise and discard the intelligence of the intelligent."

So where does this leave the philosophers, the scholars, and the world's brilliant debaters? God has made the wisdom of this world look foolish. Since God in his wisdom saw to it that the world would never know him through human wisdom, he has used our foolish preaching to save those who believe. (1 Cor. 1:19–21)

Basically, God is telling us that being smart is not the most important thing in life. I know it feels that way when you are in school, when so much of your value seems to be measured by your grades and test scores. But in God's opposite world, He values people who use the gifts they do have more than trying to rely on the gifts they don't have.

What is your favorite thing to do? Do you feel "dumb" when you are doing your favorite thing?

What are your strengths? What are some things you are good at?

The Bible teaches us that each of us is uniquely designed with special gifts to help build God's church and His kingdom. Some of us are smart. Some of us are musical. Some of us are strong. Some of us are encouragers. Some of us are servants. None of us are mistakes. We aren't supposed to be good at everything. We are supposed to come together with other believers and use our strengths to help one another. God says that we are like a body. One of us is the hand, one is the foot, one is the caboose (that's probably me), and so on. The hand isn't designed to act like the foot, and the foot isn't designed to act like the hand (read 1 Cor. 12 and Rom. 12 for a more detailed explanation).

So be yourself. Don't be ashamed of the gifts you have or don't have. Be great at the things God gifted you to be great at. The world and God's church need your exact special gifts.

For everything else, you can rely on friends or God to make up the difference. Do you know what God says about our weaknesses? "My power works best in weakness" (2 Cor. 12:9).

"My power works best in weakness."

(2 Cor. 12:9)

We don't have to hide our weaknesses. We should celebrate them because when we are bad at something, God pours out more of His supernatural power into us. We get to experience more of Him than we would if we didn't need His help.

Now don't go tell your teachers you don't have to try because you aren't gifted at math or grammar. God will give you His ability when your ability falls short. So keep working hard. Ask God to help you where you are weak. Celebrate other people's strengths, and use your own strengths to help others, and help change the world!

I WILL BOAST ONLY IN THE LORD;

LET ALL WHO ARE HELPLESS TAKE HEART.
COME, LET US TELL OF THE LORD'S GREATNESS;

LET US EXALT HIS NAME TOGETHER.

PSALM 34:2-10

Dear Living Hope,

I want to break free of the bondage of feeling dumb. As you know, my memory comes and goes, and it is especially hard for me to feel smart. I know this is a lie from Satan, and he has no power over

me. I choose to focus on building up my
knowledge of Your Word, for that is
where true wisdom is found. I find my
strength and value in You, Jesus! I will
boast in Your greatness.

I PRAYED TO THE LORD, AND HE ANSWERED ME.
HE FREED ME FROM ALL MY FEARS.
THOSE WHO LOOK TO HIM FOR HELP WILL BE RADIANT WITH JOY;
NO SHADOW OF SHAME WILL DARKEN THEIR FACES.
IN MY DESPERATION I PRAYED, AND THE LORD LISTENED;
HE SAVED ME FROM ALL MY TROUBLES.

Dear Promise Keeper,

The world can pound on me, saying I'm
not good enough, not smart enough, not
pretty enough. But today I choose to
believe the truth that I am valued; I am
loved; I am wise; I am beautiful in Your
eyes. Thank You for replacing my shame
with Your radiant joy! I am not ashamed
of who You chose me to be!

TASTE AND SEE THAT THE LORD IS GOOD.

OH, THE JOYS OF THOSE WHO TAKE REFUGE IN HIM!
FEAR THE LORD, YOU HIS GODLY PEOPLE,

FOR THOSE WHO FEAR HIM WILL HAVE ALL THEY NEED.
EVEN STRONG YOUNG LIONS SOMETIMES GO HUNGRY,

BUT THOSE WHO TRUST IN THE LORD WILL LACK
NO GOOD THING.

Lord,

Thank You that those who trust in You
will lack no good thing. Thank You that
Your grace is sufficient for me, and Your
power is made perfect in my weakness.
I can even boast in my weakness of not
having a good memory or good eyesight
because that is when Your glory is revealed.
Wow, Lord, I'm smiling just saying those
words because they are so hopeful. I'm
beyond grateful that You don't look down
on my disabilities. I believe my weakness
is what draws me closer to You. I want to
live in Your confidence today. Fill me up
today with Your courage. Remind me that
because of You, I am not lacking anything!
I love who You made me to be!

Here's a tough question: What if you don't like your strengths or wish that you had someone else's strengths? There is only one person you can take that issue up with: God. He decided which gifts to give you and which to withhold. Search your heart and ask this question: Does God make mistakes? Did He make a mistake when He chose how to design you? If you are frustrated with your strengths or weaknesses, tell God about it. Write a message to Him, and give Him a chance to respond to your frustration.

Day 14

When I feel **EMBARRASSED** . . .
I'm *sheltered* by God

What emoji best describes your MOST EMBARRASSING MOMENT? Draw it here, and write a little story about what happened (Come on, your kids will want to read this someday):

Here's mine :

In middle school, I had to give a weather report in front of my class. I was terrified to even say my name in front of the class, so I practiced for hours and memorized every word. My knees were shaking as I stood in front of my peers and began to explain that rain was coming in the forecast. For extra credit points, I brought some props and planned to open an umbrella. But as I lifted the umbrella over my head, it got hooked on my skirt. Not only did the umbrella go over my head, so did my skirt. I wanted to melt into the floor! But much to everyone's surprise, I was wearing shorts under my skirt! Ha ha! God is good! Life is crazy, but God is good!

The best thing about embarrassing moments is that they pass. They don't last forever. Only the great love and protection of our God lasts forever.

Another good thing about embarrassing moments is that they happen to everyone sooner or later. When someone you love has an embarrassing moment, put your arm around that person, and tell him or her about a time when you were embarrassed. You can have a good laugh together.

If you are the one feeling embarrassed, keep in mind that God says laughter is like good medicine (Prov. 17:22).

You are just providing free medicine for everyone. Next time you do something embarrassing, take a bow!

> Dear Heavenly Daddy,
>
> Help me run to You and hold nothing back when I am embarrassed. I know some situations can be so embarrassing, but that is not who I am. Help me break free from putting my security in my circumstances. My security is anchored in You and in who You are. Thank You for being my refuge and my safe haven. I find my confidence in Your Word and in spending time with You!

THOSE WHO LIVE IN THE SHELTER OF THE MOST HIGH
    WILL FIND REST IN THE SHADOW OF THE ALMIGHTY.
THIS I DECLARE ABOUT THE LORD:
HE ALONE IS MY REFUGE, MY PLACE OF SAFETY;
    HE IS MY GOD, AND I TRUST HIM.

PSALM 91:1–4, 9–11

> Dear Comforter,
>
> Help me realize that my value is not attached to my embarrassing moments. You are the God of second chances. You always give me a do-over. Thank You for

filling me with Your courage to seek for more. I don't want to limit how I view myself because of my circumstances. I refuse to listen to Satan's reminders of times I messed up or made mistakes. I choose to put my hope and security in Your truth, where I can find complete rest. I love that I don't have to win Your favor or impress You with my achievements. I don't have to be on a sports team or the honor roll at school. You are already proud of who I am. You love me. There is no one else like me!

FOR HE WILL RESCUE YOU FROM EVERY TRAP
AND PROTECT YOU FROM DEADLY DISEASE.
HE WILL COVER YOU WITH HIS FEATHERS.
HE WILL SHELTER YOU WITH HIS WINGS.
HIS FAITHFUL PROMISES ARE YOUR ARMOR AND
PROTECTION.

Faithful Father,

Thank You for the confidence You give me through Your Word. Scripture is my armor, my protection against the fiery darts and lies of Satan. You have given me everything I need to protect me: the shield of faith, the breastplate of righteousness, the belt of truth, the helmet of salvation, the shoes of peace, and the sword of the Spirit (Eph. 6:13–17). I love how the armor of God equips me from head to toe. The only offensive weapon is the sword of the Spirit, which is the Word of God. That is how I can defeat the enemy by quoting God's Word out loud at Satan, and he will flee. Thank You for protecting me from Satan and his schemes.

IF YOU MAKE THE LORD YOUR REFUGE,

IF YOU MAKE THE MOST HIGH YOUR SHELTER

. . . .

HE WILL ORDER HIS ANGELS

TO PROTECT YOU WHEREVER YOU GO.

Dear Mighty One,

Thank You for the promise that I'm not going through life on my own. May I never forget I have an army of angels fighting for me and defending me. Angels are com-

manded by You, and You love me so
much You send angels to comfort and
protect me. Angels fight against Satan in
the heavenly realms that I can't even see.
That is beyond incredible!

Try taking this action step: ask a parent or grandparent about his or her most embarrassing moment. Laughing with someone else will make you feel better and bring joy to your soul.

Now that your most embarrassing moment is over, what would you say to your embarrassed self? Take a few minutes to journal a prayer to God about how He sheltered your heart:

Day 15

When I feel **EXCITED** . . .
I'm *grateful*

What is the most exciting thing that happened to you this week?

Who or what made your most exciting thing possible?

Do you think of God as exciting? Put an *X* where God falls on the spectrum of boring to exciting, as you've perceived Him. Be honest.

BORING _____ *EXCITING*

If God is just someone you talk to when you open this devotional or at church once a week, chances are He might not seem very exciting to you. That's okay. Be honest. You are experiencing all kinds of fun things for the first time in your life right now. You can't see God or touch Him, so sometimes He might not even feel real to you. But I want to share a secret with you: You can "see" God through His creation, and you can "touch" Him through your prayers.

My hope is to open your eyes to something maybe you've never really thought about before. Have you ever really thought about the source of your emotions, including excitement? Who made it possible for you to have breath in your lungs to scream because your parents just gave you your favorite concert tickets? Who gave you the ability to win the game or break a team record? Who gave you the resources to go shopping and find the

> **"Whatever is good and perfect is *a gift* coming down to us from God our Father."**
>
> (James 1:17)

cutest outfit of all time? Who moved the teacher's heart to postpone the test? James 1:17 says, "Whatever is good and perfect is *a gift* coming down to us from God our Father."

The reason we get to feel excited is because of the goodness and faithfulness of our Heavenly Father. Every good and exciting thing originates with Him.

Check out the lyrics of Psalm 100. Don't worry—it's not boring. It's a very short song. Try to discover the answer to these two questions as you read: *What is God like?* and *What should I do in response to who God is and what He does for me?*

SHOUT WITH JOY TO THE LORD, ALL THE EARTH!
    WORSHIP THE LORD WITH GLADNESS.
    COME BEFORE HIM, SINGING WITH JOY.
ACKNOWLEDGE THAT THE LORD IS GOD!
    HE MADE US, AND WE ARE HIS.
    WE ARE HIS PEOPLE, THE SHEEP OF HIS PASTURE.
ENTER HIS GATES WITH THANKSGIVING;
    GO INTO HIS COURTS WITH PRAISE.
    GIVE THANKS TO HIM AND PRAISE HIS NAME.
FOR THE LORD IS GOOD.

HIS UNFAILING LOVE CONTINUES FOREVER, AND HIS FAITHFULNESS CONTINUES TO EACH GENERATION.

Next time you feel excited, stop and thank God for His good and perfect gift. Take time to recognize where it came from, and be grateful. Your gratitude will literally open the doors of God's throne room to you, where you can stand in His presence and experience even more exciting adventures that flow from being near Him (v. 4).

Dear Lover of My Soul,

You are writing my story. Each day is an adventure with You. I often want to skip ahead a few chapters: Will I get married? Will my thyroid cancer be completely healed? Will my memory improve? But the excitement is in not knowing what will happen next. The beauty comes in trusting Your perfect plan and waiting on Your perfect timing to unwrap it for me. All I can do is praise You and shout, "Thank You" as loud as I can. Thank You for knowing my name. Thank You that I am not my own. Daddy, I am Yours. I am Your daughter. Thank You that I know the secret to life: it's a relationship with You!

Thank You that this world is not my home.
Thank you that I will see You in heaven
one day, where the party.is just getting
started, and the best is yet to come!

Here's a challenge: Psalm 100:3 says to "acknowledge that the LORD is God." Another way of saying that is to invite God to engage in your favorite activities with You. Be aware of His presence in everything you do. Or simply take time to say "thank You" to God whenever something exciting happens.

God is never boring. If you haven't experienced how fun and exciting He is, ask Him to show you. What do you love to do? If you are artistic, draw a picture that depicts for God what happened at school today, or paint your favorite verse in the Bible. If you like music, write a praise song to Jesus, or make up a dance routine to go with your favorite praise song. If you like nature, walk barefoot in the grass or stream, and talk to God about your day. If you like to journal, write your own poem about how you see God in the world around you. You could even make a video, or take pictures of your favorite scenery outside that makes you happy. If you love people, throw a party, and ask God to be your guest of honor; make it the best party ever!

Day 16

When I feel **FAT** . . .
I'm just the *right size*
for my destiny!

After my big accident, I had the incredible honor of speaking at a national cheerleading banquet to nearly a thousand cheerleaders. I could no longer be on a competition cheer team because of my injuries, but I could share my miracle story and invite girls to be a cheerleader for Jesus!

I was so excited! I had on a gorgeous, form-fitting, formal gown in iridescent bronze with sequins from the bodice to the floor. I remember riding to the event with my mom and my grandmother (I call her "Nanny"). I was riding in the front passenger seat and feeling like Cinderella. Everything was going like a dream until . . . I let out an unexpected sneeze and—POP!

It was the zipper on the back of my dress! Due to my new physical limitations, I had gained a few pounds and the zipper had ripped away from the dress! Nightmare!

Immediately I said out loud, "Satan, you are going to have to do more than that to keep me from speaking tonight in this dress!" By the literal grace of God, my mom just happened to have a little sewing kit in her purse. We stood outside in the drizzling rain as Nanny sewed up the back of my dress before anyone saw me. The best part of the story is this: because I had brain damage and very little short-term memory, I was able to forget the entire drama and walk right onto that stage like nothing had ever happened! God gave me His perfect words in the perfect moment, and I was able to proclaim the mighty name of Jesus from the stage in front of a thousand young girls.

The victory is worth whatever feelings we have to battle to get there. God always wins. He always restores joy. I was just the right size for God to use me for His glory! Plus, we have a great laugh every time we retell this story!

Every girl (young or old) feels fat at times. Have you ever stopped to consider that *fat* is relative? I mean, it totally depends on who or what you are comparing yourself to. Would you feel fat if you were standing next to a supermodel? What about if she was pregnant? She would, of course, need to get bigger to give birth to new life.

Would you feel fat standing next to a Sumo wrestler? Yet he needs to be his large size to win! A swimmer needs a different body from the one a gymnast needs. Actresses have to be different sizes to fit different roles. Lots of body shapes and sizes are needed for the world to work!

Have you ever thought about who decides what *fat* is? What is the imaginary line you can or can't cross and not feel fat? There is so much pressure today to be a certain weight or height, or to fit into certain clothes. God wants to focus on our hearts. That is what He is measuring. How *fat* is your heart for God? For other people? For changing the world?

I would have missed a great opportunity to share Jesus if I had focused on my dress ripping or feeling fat instead of my purpose. Let's break free from the bondage of fitting into a stereotype of what others think of us! Let's pray through our *fat* feelings together! Ready? Repeat after me:

Dear Loving God,

Help me know that I don't have to look perfect or act perfect. No one is perfect. Only Jesus is perfect. Help me know You are proud of me. You delight in me, and I am beautiful because You made me and You don't make mistakes.

I ENVIED THE PROUD

. . . .

THEY SEEM TO LIVE SUCH PAINLESS LIVES;
   THEIR BODIES ARE SO HEALTHY AND STRONG.
THEY DON'T HAVE TROUBLES LIKE OTHER PEOPLE;
   THEY'RE NOT PLAGUED WITH PROBLEMS LIKE
      EVERYONE ELSE.

PSALM 73:3–5, 21–28

Dear Creator of the Universe,

I don't ever want to label myself again as
fat. Help me focus on my inner beauty
instead of my outer beauty. People might
look at my outward appearance, but You
look at my heart (1 Sam. 16:7). Father,
Your Word says You search the whole
earth looking for a heart completely
surrendered to You (2 Chron. 16:9). If
I am sold out to Your purpose, then
You will use me in ways I never dreamed
possible! Help me focus more on my heart
than on my body! You don't search for the
right body; Father, You search for the right
heart! Please forgive me for falling into the
comparison trap. Forgive me for looking at

social media and feeling inadequate. Forgive me for wanting to look like other girls instead of celebrating who I am in You. Comparison is the thief of my joy, Jesus. You died so that I could have victory and joy. You came to give me life to the fullest!

THEN I REALIZED THAT MY HEART WAS BITTER,
    AND I WAS ALL TORN UP INSIDE.
I WAS SO FOOLISH AND IGNORANT—
    I MUST HAVE SEEMED LIKE A SENSELESS ANIMAL
        TO YOU.

Jesus,

You enjoyed eating on this earth. Teach me how to eat to be healthy and strong. I don't want to be consumed with eating too much or not eating enough. I want to have energy and have balance in my eating. Jesus, I want to enjoy life. Give me Your balance and discipline when it comes to eating so I can enjoy food and also have some boundaries when it comes to unhealthy food choices. I don't want to be controlled by food; instead, I want to be controlled by your Spirit who lives in me.

YET I STILL BELONG TO YOU;
YOU HOLD MY RIGHT HAND.
YOU GUIDE ME WITH YOUR COUNSEL,
LEADING ME TO A GLORIOUS DESTINY.
WHOM HAVE I IN HEAVEN BUT YOU?
I DESIRE YOU MORE THAN ANYTHING ON EARTH.

Holy Spirit,

Thank You that my body is Your dwelling place. Help me take good care of Your home. Eating disorders are a serious problem. I pray against Satan and any evil plan he has to make me think I have to be thinner to be liked or a certain size to fit in. Help me focus on having a beautiful heart. That is what truly matters to You. God, You made me this size to fulfill my destiny and the amazing plan You have for me. I trust You have a good plan for my life. Lord, use my size to make a difference in the world!

MY HEALTH MAY FAIL, AND MY SPIRIT MAY GROW WEAK,
BUT GOD REMAINS THE STRENGTH OF MY HEART;
HE IS MINE FOREVER.

. . . .

BUT AS FOR ME, HOW GOOD IT IS TO BE NEAR GOD!
I HAVE MADE THE SOVEREIGN LORD MY SHELTER,
AND I WILL TELL EVERYONE ABOUT THE WONDERFUL
THINGS YOU DO.

Holy Father,

May Your voice be the loudest voice I
hear! Your opinion is the most important.
Lord, I want to be happy, healthy, and
strong. I have so much pressure to fit
in, to achieve, to please my parents, to
be good. All of that pressure can lead to
eating problems. I want to break free of
weight bondage. I want to see myself the
way You see me. Give me victory over my
fat feelings and fears. Give me victory in
Jesus' name!

Day 17

When I feel **INVISIBLE** ...
I'm *seen* and *known*

Most of the psalms we have been reading together were written by King David. He was *the most famous* and definitely *the most popular* king Israel ever had. In fact, he is still considered a celebrity by most Jewish people and has a city named after him.

You'll never guess what he was like when he was your age. Popular? Nope. Well liked? Nope. Voted Most Likely to Be Famous? Nope.

He was invisible!

As a young teenager, David was so overlooked by his own family that when the prophet Samuel came to his house and asked Jesse (David's father) to line up all of his sons because God had chosen one of them to be the next king, he didn't even put David in the lineup! Samuel looked at all seven of David's older, handsome, championship brothers, and God told him to keep passing by each one. God explained to Samuel, "The LORD doesn't see things the way you see them. People judge by outward appearance, but the LORD looks at the heart" (1 Sam. 16:7).

Finally Samuel asked Jesse if there were any more sons. Jesse replied, "Only the youngest, but he isn't very important. He looks kind of ruddy. We send him out to watch the sheep and goats."

Samuel commanded the family to get that absent youngest son, and when the invisible, overlooked David walked in, God said, "He's the one. I choose him. I have seen him. I have heard him. He has been out in the hills writing songs about Me. Make him the next king because he is the one who has a heart like Mine."

David still had to wait a few years in hiding before he became king at age thirty. During the first three decades of his life, he was mostly invisible and overlooked. Yet he wrote these beautiful lyrics about being seen and heard by a God who faithfully loved him.

If you feel invisible, know that God sees you. He hears you. He knows everything about you, and He is crazy about you! You don't have to worry about who notices you or understands you. You only have to worry about being seen and heard by God. Spend your energy developing a heart like His. Then God will make you seen and known by just the right people at just the right time. Focus on your love relationship with God for now; let Him take care of the rest later. That's how David became Israel's greatest leader.

Read David's lyrics from Psalm 33, and rewrite them in your own words, or make an attempt to interpret what you think they mean.

THE LORD LOOKS DOWN FROM HEAVEN
    AND SEES THE WHOLE HUMAN RACE.
FROM HIS THRONE HE OBSERVES
    ALL WHO LIVE ON THE EARTH.
HE MADE THEIR HEARTS,
    SO HE UNDERSTANDS EVERYTHING THEY DO.

PSALM 33:13–23

Rephrase that much in your own words:

BUT THE LORD WATCHES OVER THOSE WHO FEAR HIM,
THOSE WHO RELY ON HIS UNFAILING LOVE.
HE RESCUES THEM FROM DEATH
AND KEEPS THEM ALIVE IN TIMES OF FAMINE.

In your words:

WE PUT OUR HOPE IN THE LORD.
HE IS OUR HELP AND OUR SHIELD.
IN HIM OUR HEARTS REJOICE,
FOR WE TRUST IN HIS HOLY NAME.
LET YOUR UNFAILING LOVE SURROUND US, LORD,
FOR OUR HOPE IS IN YOU ALONE.

In your words:

Based on your interpretation of Psalm 33, what is one good piece of advice you could share with a friend when he or she is feeling invisible:

Priceless

Dear Heavenly Father,

You see me from the inside out. You even see the scars hidden on my heart that no one else can see. I can't begin to fathom Your love for me. Thank You for pursuing me and healing my heart a little more each day. Daddy, I want to put this feeling of being invisible totally behind me because I know I am chosen and redeemed. I am a daughter of the King! Thank You for bending down from heaven to see me and hear me.

Day 18

When I feel **LEFT OUT** . . .
I'm *chosen* by God

In sixth grade, I used to feel like a third wheel. Two of my friends would whisper and laugh and leave me out of their conversations. They were my friends when it was convenient or if one of them wasn't there. Whenever one of them was sick and absent from school, then I was the other's favorite person. But when all three of us were together, I was constantly feeling left out. For a whole year, I tried to get them to like me. I wanted to fit in. Then one day I opened my eyes and realized there was a really sweet, fun girl sitting right next to me in class. She was new to our school and needed a friend. I started focusing on being her friend instead of focusing on how I was being left out. I was so much happier when I tried to be a friend instead of waiting for others to befriend me.

That time in my life happened before Instagram and Snapchat revolutionized the world. Today the temptation to focus on feeling left out is even greater because you are surrounded by constant images on social media reminding you that you weren't invited or your friends are having fun without you.

My cousin is closer to your age. One summer, she was feeling left out of her friend group and her mom kept telling her to invite the neighbor girl to hang out. My cousin kept seeing pictures on Instagram of the neighbor girl at the beach and told her mom, "She doesn't want to hang out with me. She's not even home; she's been at the beach with friends all summer." Later my aunt ran into the neighbor girl's mom, who confided that her daughter was having a really lonely summer and was stuck at home by herself every day. My aunt said, "I thought she's been at the beach?" The neighbor girl's mom replied that she kept posting old pictures of spring break at the beach because she didn't want everyone to know she was home alone with nothing to do! All that summer, the two of them could have been hanging out! They were less than a hundred feet apart and both needing a friend. Social media never tells the whole story!

When you feel left out, take the focus off yourself. Look for someone worse off than you. Focus on making that person feel special, and you will feel better too. The cure for being left out is finding purpose.

While you are trying to find a new purpose, take comfort in the truth that God has chosen you! He "delights in you" and calls you His "special possession." Pay close attention to these words, and underline the words that make you feel special.

HE REACHED DOWN FROM HEAVEN AND RESCUED ME;
    HE DREW ME OUT OF DEEP WATERS.
HE RESCUED ME FROM MY POWERFUL ENEMIES,
    FROM THOSE WHO HATED ME AND WERE TOO STRONG
      FOR ME.
THEY ATTACKED ME AT A MOMENT WHEN I WAS IN DISTRESS,
    BUT THE LORD SUPPORTED ME.
HE LED ME TO A PLACE OF SAFETY;
    HE RESCUED ME BECAUSE HE DELIGHTS IN ME.

PSALM 18:16–19

THE LORD WILL NOT REJECT HIS PEOPLE;
    HE WILL NOT ABANDON HIS SPECIAL POSSESSION.

PSALM 94:14

Dear Best Friend,

Thank You for reminding me that I am never left out with You, Jesus. You are always waiting for me to talk to You. Lord, I am so sorry for all the times I have left You out of my schedule. There are many days I didn't stop to spend time with You. I wonder how it makes You feel when You have done everything for me and I don't even notice that You are beside me, holding my hand. Please forgive me for being so busy and distracted that I forget the most important thing—spending time with You! Lord, I love the image of You reaching down from heaven and rescuing me. It reminds me that You chose me! You had Your eye on me, and You reached down and picked me! Wow! Thank You for choosing me! Lord, the truth is I don't want to blend in. I want to be a light in the darkness. I'm not afraid to be different. I want to be an encouragement and give hope to others. Jesus, I want to get out of the boat and walk on water with You just like Peter did in the Bible. Give me the courage to try the impossible and to keep my eyes focused on You.

Excerpt from my high school journal before my accident:

> Why would anyone desire to become like the world? It just doesn't make sense. Lord, I am not going to blend in because I know I was born to stand out! To stand alone? Maybe (if that's what it takes). . . . So God, pretty much I am begging You to use me. Father, I know You take the foolish ones, the weak ones, the lowly people and use them to shame the strong and the wise. God, so that means You can take me just as I am (1 Cor. 1:26–27 NIV). You can take me, a nobody, and turn me into a somebody. Take this year and my life and allow Your glory to shine. Take it, and use it to its fullest potential!

Try writing your own journal entry to God about how you feel today:

HERE ARE SOME ACTION STEPS
FOR WHEN YOU FEEL LEFT OUT:

1. *Sit by someone different at lunch.*

2. *Smile and say, "Hi" to five people you don't know.*

3. *Invite a new friend over to your house.*

4. *Only use positive comments that build others up when you're on social media.*

Day 19

When I feel like **CRYING** . . .
I'm *comforted* by God

Have you ever had something you liked to collect? Maybe dolls, stuffed animals, quarters from all fifty states, or T-shirts from around the world? Anything come to mind? Growing up, I used to collect buttons, colored rocks, and seashells. I even used to collect the empty toilet-paper rolls out of the trash can to make them into one of my fun and funky creations. Ha! I'll bet no one has ever had such an odd collection as that!

Sketch a picture of your collection:

On a scale of 1–10 (10 being super-duper), how special was your collection to you while you were still trying hard to collect it all?

1 2 3 4 5 6 7 8 9 10

Where did you keep your collection?

Did you take good care of it or panic when someone tried to harm it?

Did you know that God has a collection in heaven? Can you guess what He collects? _____

Psalm 56:8 says, "You keep track of all my sorrows. You have collected all my tears in your bottle. You have recorded each one in your book."

God collects your tears! He keeps them in a special, safe place, His bottle. And just to be extra sure He does not lose a single one, He also records them in His book! Every single one of your tears matters to God. Whether you have big reasons to cry or no reason to cry and tears flow anyway, God collects them all—each and every one!

Why is God so careful to collect your tears? First, because He promises to wipe every tear from your eye when you get to heaven (Rev. 21:4). Someday, you will never feel like crying again. For all of eternity, you will never ever feel sad. God will make sure you know that He saw every tear and He kept every tear just so He could make each one go away forever!

And second, God has promised never to waste a tear or a trial. God will find a way to use every single one of your tears for your own good and the good of others (Rom. 8:28).

So what do you do in the meantime on the days that you feel like crying? Do what Jesus did. The Bible tells us that "Jesus wept" (John 11:35). The word for *wept* doesn't just mean a few trickle tears; it means He did the full-fledged ugly cry! Jesus' tears were seen by the people around Him that day; they saw His compassion and His heartbreak. His example demonstrates to us that it's absolutely okay to cry. So let the tears come! Don't hold them back anymore!

Let's pray through Psalm 42 together.

DAY AND NIGHT I HAVE ONLY TEARS FOR FOOD

. . . .

MY HEART IS BREAKING
      AS I REMEMBER HOW IT USED TO BE.

Dear Almighty Healer,

You know, Father, that I used to have a totally different personality. School and reading are so much harder now. I can't play sports anymore. I'll never drive a car (unless You choose to miraculously heal my vision). I have had to make new friends. It can be hard, but I want to embrace and discover the new me—the new dreams, desires, and passions You have placed in my heart because of the hard things I have had to endure. You have new things for me to do! You promise never to waste one of my tears. Use my story to give hope to others.

Dear Almighty Healer,

It can be very sad and bring tears to my eyes when I think about (Write your own difficulty here!):

WHY AM I DISCOURAGED?
   WHY IS MY HEART SO SAD?
I WILL PUT MY HOPE IN GOD!
   I WILL PRAISE HIM AGAIN—
   MY SAVIOR AND MY GOD!
NOW I AM DEEPLY DISCOURAGED,
   BUT I WILL REMEMBER YOU . . .

Forgive me for having tears of self-pity. I want
to trust in You. Lord, I don't want to limit
You in any way. When my heart is sad and I
am overwhelmed with difficult circumstances,

help me not to forget everything You have done for me. Wow! There is victory when I remember that there is no one else like me. I choose to trust that You will turn my mourning into dancing. I may cry today, but new joy will come in the morning!

EACH DAY THE LORD POURS HIS UNFAILING LOVE UPON ME, AND THROUGH EACH NIGHT I SING HIS SONGS, PRAYING TO GOD WHO GIVES ME LIFE.

Thank You that discouragement does not have Your name on it, for You are a God of encouragement. I don't ever want to forget who You are. For You are life and love. You are glorious, wonderful, unfailing, and everything I need. You are my healer, my comforter, and my best friend!

Write out the words to Psalm 42:8 in your own handwriting:

According to this verse, what can help you get through the times when you feel like crying?

Here's a helpful tip: when I was recovering from my accident, I could not get dressed in the morning or ride in a car without crying because of the physical pain and dizziness. My friends and family started playing praise music for me, and those songs helped me survive. The praise music was the only thing that kept me from crying. Try listening to your favorite worship songs on Spotify or Pandora next time you feel like crying. I promise it helps!

Day 20

When I feel like **DANCING** ...
I'm making God *smile*

What would it take for you to jump up in front of a bunch
of people and dance your little heart out?

- A notification that you got a 100 on your
  science exam?

- A voicemail saying you got the lead role in your
  favorite musical? (and you could actually sing)

- An announcement that you just won a free
  year's supply of your favorite fast food?

- An invitation to go to the Olympics to compete
  in the sport of your choice?

- A text message from your favorite celebrity offering you backstage passes to his or her show this weekend?

How about news that your Heavenly Father will wipe every tear from your eye and every sorrow from your soul? Did you know that God promises to turn your sadness into dancing ALWAYS!?!

When I was learning to walk again after being in a coma for five weeks, I felt like crying every time I had to stand up. Everything hurt so bad. My brain injury caused my feelings to be magnified so that a little pain felt like torture! The only way my physical therapist could get me to stand up and practice walking was to tell me that it was "Dancing Day." He knew I loved to dance, so he would turn my praise music on, put my arms around his neck and ask me to dance with him. That's how I learned to walk again—by dancing.

Dancing can happen in your heart even when your body can't move. That's when you are overflowing with love for your Savior. We all dance in different ways. It can be singing, humming, drawing a picture, playing a musical instrument, or doing the latest line dance. Dancing comes with that feeling of exuberance, when you are overtaken with awe and reverence for God. It's your soul talking. You never want the moment to end. You forget everything else except your love for your Savior.

That dancing moment came for King David the day he danced in the streets. Something sad had happened, making him feel as if God were distant. Then, when God finally turned his sorrow into joy, David's soul overflowed with worship to God, and he danced before God—and a whole lot of other people—with all his might. Later David wrote this song about that kind of moment.

WEEPING MAY STAY FOR THE NIGHT,
    BUT REJOICING COMES IN THE MORNING.

. . . .

YOU TURNED MY WAILING INTO DANCING;
    YOU REMOVED MY SACKCLOTH AND CLOTHED ME WITH JOY.

Dear Magnificent One,

Whenever I think of dancing, it reminds me of heaven and what is to come. I can't wait to dance on streets of gold with all the angels and sing forever and ever, "Holy, Holy, Holy are You, Lord God Almighty. The whole earth is filled with Your glory." I am going to shout Your name as loud as I can. It is better than a dream. It is THE dream to be with You one day, face-to-face, where there is no pain and no suffering!

I can only imagine!

THAT MY HEART MAY SING YOUR PRAISES AND NOT BE SILENT. LORD MY GOD, I WILL PRAISE YOU FOREVER.

Dear Great I AM,

I lift up all my praise and adoration to You. Thank You for times of weeping and mourning, so I get the privilege of watching You reverse it to dancing. Thank You, Daddy, for how you take the broken pieces of my life and turn me into Your masterpiece. You transform my pain into purpose. I will never be shaken!

Here's a fun Dare (with a capital *D*): Go turn on your praise music, blare it loud, and dance your heart out (with or without people watching). Have fun! Watch how contagious your worship can be. I'll bet you'll catch someone smiling at you. At the very least, your Heavenly Father will be grinning ear to ear.

When I feel like **GIVING UP** … I'm about to be *rescued*

When I was in third grade, I wrecked my bike in our neighborhood. My leg was bleeding, and I was crying. I couldn't walk. I just sat there on the pavement and gravel while my little brother raced home on his bike with training wheels to get my dad. About twenty minutes later, my dad picked me up in his arms and carried me home. I will never forget the feeling I had of being rescued—safe and secure—in my father's arms.

That is exactly how you can feel in your Heavenly Father's arms. He promises to carry you and rescue you. Don't ever give up. Isaiah 46:4 says, "I have made you and I will carry you; I will sustain you and I will rescue you" (NIV).

There have been many times since the third grade that I felt like giving up. At the age of fifteen, I had to relearn how to walk, talk, read, write, eat, and even breathe on my own without a ventilator. Imagine not being able to write your name as a teenager! Every time I felt like giving up, I would stop and *praise God in advance* for rescuing me. Literally, to just stand up, I would say, "Thank You, Father, for raising me up. I know I can do all things through You." What I was doing was creating a new pathway in my brain to override the old one that was damaged.

One thing I have learned while recovering from a brain injury is that YOU ARE THE BOSS OF YOUR BRAIN. Most of the time, our brains operate on autopilot. For example, you don't have to tell your brain to breathe while you sleep or to scream when you see a giant cockroach. But you can override autopilot mode if you choose to by telling your brain what to do. Your brain will believe whatever you tell it to believe, because you are the BOSS!

Our feelings also come from autopilot mode. We don't wake up and say, "Today I want to feel sad," and suddenly we feel sad. No, we wake up with a feeling, and then we have to tell our brains what to believe about that feeling. That's why it's so important to bring our feelings to God and His Word to see what He says is true about our feelings.

145

If you are 100 percent honest, how do you feel right now?

Thank you for being honest. What you feel is real. But just because the feelings are real doesn't make them *true*. Today, you might feel like giving up because your brain believes you are failing or God is failing you. The truth is God will never fail you, and He plans to carry you and rescue you during this tough time. You have to tell your brain that truth, and you do that by praying Scripture out loud and declaring who God is.

Psalm 107 tells the story of some people who felt like giving up. At first, all they could pray was, "Lord, help!" It was a good start to turn to God when they found themselves on the brink of quitting. Sometimes we get so overwhelmed by our feelings or circumstances, all we can say is "Lord, help!" After a while though, these people were able go from begging for help to praising "the LORD for his great love." They were starting to speak the truth to their feelings. They were becoming the boss of their brains. You can do it too!

SOME WANDERED IN THE WILDERNESS,
  LOST AND HOMELESS.
HUNGRY AND THIRSTY,
  THEY NEARLY DIED.
"LORD, HELP!" THEY CRIED IN THEIR TROUBLE,
  AND HE RESCUED THEM FROM THEIR DISTRESS.
HE LED THEM STRAIGHT TO SAFETY,
  TO A CITY WHERE THEY COULD LIVE.
LET THEM PRAISE THE LORD FOR HIS GREAT LOVE
  AND FOR THE WONDERFUL THINGS HE HAS DONE FOR THEM.
FOR HE SATISFIES THE THIRSTY
  AND FILLS THE HUNGRY WITH GOOD THINGS.

Now try being the boss of your brain. Tell your brain the truth about how you are feeling. Include some truth about who God is and what He has done for you before (write that below). See if you can change from begging to praising!

And here's a bright idea: What if you could visually *see* God at work? Would that help you not want to give up? What I do is write my prayer requests on different bright-colored sticky notes and stick them on the back of the door in my bedroom. When God answers that request or rescues me from that problem, I move the colored sticky note to a different wall across my room. This gives me a bright visual reminder that God is real and that He answers prayer. It helps me to *see* that He is at work in my life.

And here's an even brighter idea: When I pray, I say, "God, do this or something GREATER!" I don't want to limit God to my plans. I want to see His supernatural miracles that my mind can't even imagine!

I'M ABOUT TO BE *rescued*

Dear All-Powerful One,

Life can be hard. Help me remember
You want to come to my rescue and You
promise to take me to a place of safety.
You are my safe haven. I can find rest even
when all I can cry out to You is "Jesus,
help!" You meet me right where I am, and
You give me hope. Just saying Your name
out loud fills my heart with new hope. I
put all my expectations in You. I want to
change my brain today from feeling hope-
less to feeling hopeful. I know you have an
amazing purpose for my life, and I don't
want to miss one plan You have for me!
With Your strength, I can do the impossible,
Lord. Today I choose to tap into Your
power that lives in me. Empty me of all my
anxiety and fears, and fill me with Your
supernatural power. Thank You for helping
me make it through one more day. Do
this, or something GREATER, Lord. You
are the great I AM!

When I feel like **LAUGHING** ...
I'm *praising* God

Have you ever laughed so hard that you

- Fell to the floor

- Snorted really loud

- Pulled a stomach muscle

- Accidentally wet your pants

- All of the above

When was the last time you remember laughing that hard? What happened?

What is the funniest movie you have ever seen?

Which one of your friends or family members makes you laugh the most?

Would you rather laugh for thirty minutes with friends or get a pedicure alone?

Would you rather watch a funny romantic comedy or a scary movie that makes you scream?

Have you ever been in a situation where you were supposed to be quiet but you couldn't stop laughing? What happened?

Laughter isn't controllable. You can't control how long or short your laugh attack might be. It's your soul talking instead of your brain.

Like salvation, laughter is a free gift from God. It's God's best natural medicine. I've learned from browsing on the internet that

- Laughter makes you feel better (it releases endorphins that trigger feelings of happiness).

- Laughter helps you cope with anxiety (it decreases stress hormones).

- Laughter fights disease (it increases your immune system).

- Laughter burns calories (it goes great with ice cream. I didn't need the internet for that one!)

My mom and I have always had this silly tradition of laughing after we eat a big meal. Whenever we feel miserably full, we go lie on the bed and laugh together. It's like we literally laugh it off.

We have the choice every day to focus on the positive or the negative. Who would you rather spend time with—someone who is lighthearted and looks for reasons to laugh, or someone who's always negative and complaining?

One of my favorite things to do with my mom is laugh. Even when we went through our darkest times, we found things to laugh about. One time in the hospital when I was waking up from my coma, the therapist asked me, "Jen, what can fly, a bird or an elephant?" I answered, "Elephant." I honestly didn't know the answer. The pathways in my brain were so jumbled up. I don't remember doing it, but my mom said I started quacking like a duck. At first, she wanted to cry because she was so sad that I couldn't even answer preschool questions, but when she saw me acting like a duck in my full-grown body, she just had to laugh! I think she even started quacking too, just for the fun of it!

We don't get to choose our hardships, but we do get to choose how we will walk through them. I choose laughter.

A huge part of our relationship with God is to praise Him. Praise happens when our hearts are so full of God that they overflow with some kind of outward response— singing, praying, dancing, even laughing. Laughter is one of the best ways to praise God. Joy speaks out loud when we laugh. The more we lose control through laughter, the more God's Spirit takes over.

Next to my bed on my nightstand I have a picture of Jesus laughing. We often think of Jesus as being a teacher or being serious or suffering on the cross. But I like to think of Jesus laughing, not at me but with me. Jesus is fun and exciting. He is alive! He is my best friend, and He is never boring. I love spending time with Him!

WE WERE FILLED WITH LAUGHTER,
    AND WE SANG FOR JOY.
AND THE OTHER NATIONS SAID,
    "WHAT AMAZING THINGS THE LORD HAS DONE FOR THEM."
YES, THE LORD HAS DONE AMAZING THINGS FOR US!
    WHAT JOY!

PSALM 126:2-6

Priceless

Dear Miraculous One,

I am grinning from ear to ear. I just want to say thank You for laughter. When I laugh it gives my soul a way to talk. Laughter spills out when I can't contain my joy any longer. Laughter lifts up my heart. I have never met anyone who is mad or angry who is also laughing. Thank You for the private jokes between You and me that no one else knows. Thank You for noticing silly things about me that no one else sees. Thank You for doing things that only I would notice and value. You do those things because You know they are important to me and bring such joy to my heart. No one gets me like You, Lord!

RESTORE OUR FORTUNES, LORD,
    AS STREAMS RENEW THE DESERT.
THOSE WHO PLANT IN TEARS
    WILL HARVEST WITH SHOUTS OF JOY.
THEY WEEP AS THEY GO TO PLANT THEIR SEED,
    BUT THEY SING AS THEY RETURN WITH THE HARVEST.

Daddy,

I want to be filled with laughter that radiates You and Your glory. I believe You want us to enjoy life because life is short. Help me to be able to laugh no matter what hard things I face. Remind me that everything that makes me sad will end, but joy will last forever! When I think about heaven, I can't help but laugh. I want to celebrate with You forever!

Here's a theory: laughter is contagious!

Choose one of the following experiments:

- Get a table of your friends or family to laugh really loud in public, and count how many heads turn and smile at you.

- Have a staring contest with someone, and dare him or her not to crack a smile. See how long it takes for both of you to start laughing.

- Smile at ten randomly chosen people today, and count how many smile back.

Day 23

When I feel like **SINGING** . . .
I'm *energized*

Do you have any secret hiding places in your room? Think about your most prized possession. Where do you keep it? Do you have a jewelry box, a safe place for childhood memories, or a hidden compartment where you hide your money?

Did you know your brain has secret hiding places? For example, *songs* are stored in a more protected part of your brain than other memories are. The last thing I did before my brain got damaged in a car accident was sing my favorite praise song with my high school choir at church. I loved that song. I did not have a soloist voice by any stretch of the imagination, but that didn't stop me from singing it 24/7.

When I woke up from a five-week coma, my brain was injured in so many places I didn't even recognize my family. But guess what I remembered? That song! I couldn't say or write my name. I couldn't tell you any colors or numbers. But I knew every word to that praise song hidden away in a secret place of my brain!

Even though my mind and my body were broken, my spirit was alive and strong! I could not sit up or walk yet, but I could sing the solo on that song like I was auditioning for *The Voice*.

Songs are powerful. They are attached to emotions that are stronger than your brain. A song can make you cry, laugh, or dance for joy. When I sing, nothing else matters. All my pain fades away. I just feel pure joy, hope, and purpose. Singing energizes my spirit!

Psalms tells us God is in enthroned on the praise of His people (Ps. 22:3). That means His presence is alive and with us when we sing about who He is and what He can do. I'm saying that He actually lives in our songs! That's why you can't stay sad when you sing songs about Him. You have to smile. A power takes over your whole body that makes you feel alive and whole.

Songs =
Power

Songs + God
Living in Them =
Super Power

Singing works two ways. It can be an overflow of your inner spirit. When you are full of love and joy, you just can't help but explode in song. Or singing can be something you choose to do when you feel down or afraid. A praise song can change your mood. It can pump you up and make you courageous! Either way, God wants you to sing!

Here's what He has to say about singing.

PSALM 96:1-4

SING A NEW SONG TO THE LORD!

    LET THE WHOLE EARTH SING TO THE LORD!

SING TO THE LORD; PRAISE HIS NAME.

    EACH DAY PROCLAIM THE GOOD NEWS THAT HE SAVES.

PUBLISH HIS GLORIOUS DEEDS AMONG THE NATIONS.

    TELL EVERYONE ABOUT THE AMAZING THINGS HE DOES.

GREAT IS THE LORD! HE IS MOST WORTHY OF PRAISE!

According to this passage,

1. Who should sing? Everyone on earth or only people who can keep a tune?

2. How often should we sing? At church or every day?

3. What should we sing about? How great God is or how great you look in your jeans?

Almighty Creator,

When I sing, my troubles fade away. When I sing, my soul and body get so in tune with You, I feel Your presence. It's almost like You are reaching down from heaven and giving me a great big hug. Give me a song today that is full of You, Lord. I want to be where You are! I want to tell the world how great You are!

The songs you surround yourself with have a *huge* impact on how you feel! They are stored in a special place and will be with you for a long time. So choose your playlist carefully. It has a lot of power over you!

What three songs could you add to your playlist that would help you feel alive and whole?

1. _____

2. _____

3. _____

Experiment: Try waking up to one of these songs instead of an alarm. See if you feel happier that day.

Day 24

When I feel
MISUNDERSTOOD . . .
I'm *heard* by God

One of the most frustrating feelings on earth is to feel like no one understands you! Have you ever felt misunderstood? Maybe someone twisted something you said or did or thought you meant something you really didn't mean. Do you know the feeling?

Who seems to misunderstand you most often? (Circle as many as apply to you.)

Parents   Teachers   Teammates   Siblings

Friends   Coaches   Classmates

Other: _____

I have good news for you. Jesus felt misunderstood too! He came to earth so He could relate to every feeling you ever will feel and be able to say, "I understand! I've felt that way too!"

One time Jesus got lost from His parents for three days. He was just doing what His Heavenly Father wanted Him to do by teaching in the temple, but His earthly parents thought Jesus was being irresponsible. Can you believe it? Jesus, the King of kings and Lord of lords, was accused of being irresponsible by His earthly parents! They talked it over and worked it out but not before He experienced that feeling you've felt of not being trusted by someone you love.

Have you ever felt the powerful relief of someone saying, "I understand! I know just how you feel! I've felt that way, too!" The empathy of a friend can lift the burden right off your chest. Jesus offers that understanding! There is not a single feeling you will ever experience that Jesus did not feel too! He was your age once. He understands. When you feel misunderstood, you can talk to Him about it.

David, the author of most of the psalms, felt misunderstood too. He was trying to be a loyal helper to King Saul, but the king became jealous of him and kept trying to kill him! David took the high road and never tried to get revenge (even when he had the opportunity), but Saul still tried to hurt him. For many years, David had to run and hide in caves. It was during those years that he wrote many of the psalms we know and love today.

Read David's words out loud. Can you tell he knows what it feels like to be misunderstood?

O LORD, HEAR MY PLEA FOR JUSTICE.
    LISTEN TO MY CRY FOR HELP.
PAY ATTENTION TO MY PRAYER,
    FOR IT COMES FROM HONEST LIPS.
DECLARE ME INNOCENT,
    FOR YOU SEE THOSE WHO DO RIGHT.

YOU HAVE TESTED MY THOUGHTS AND EXAMINED MY HEART
        IN THE NIGHT.
    YOU HAVE SCRUTINIZED ME AND FOUND NOTHING WRONG.
    I AM DETERMINED NOT TO SIN IN WHAT I SAY.
I HAVE FOLLOWED YOUR COMMANDS,
    WHICH KEEP ME FROM FOLLOWING CRUEL AND EVIL PEOPLE.
MY STEPS HAVE STAYED ON YOUR PATH;
    I HAVE NOT WAVERED FROM FOLLOWING YOU.

I AM PRAYING TO YOU BECAUSE I KNOW YOU WILL ANSWER,
   O GOD.
      BEND DOWN AND LISTEN AS I PRAY.
SHOW ME YOUR UNFAILING LOVE IN WONDERFUL WAYS.

Who did David turn to for help when he felt misunderstood?

In your own handwriting, rewrite verses 6–7 as a prayer below: "I am praying to you because I know you will answer, O God. Bend down and listen as I pray. Show me your unfailing love in wonderful ways":

When people don't understand you, God knows the desires of your heart. You serve an audience of One. Focus on making God proud, and let Him take care of everyone else's opinion. He hears you. He understands you. He loves you. That's all that really matters!

Dear Lover of My Soul,

Thank You that You hear my cry for help and You pay attention to me. I feel better just talking to You, the One who knew me before I was ever born. You know my deepest desires and understand my personality. You know every secret in my heart. Wow! Lord, You know everything about me, and You still love me! I cannot believe You know my thoughts and You still declare me innocent because Jesus died for my sins on the cross. What great love. What great sacrifice. Thank You that I am free from shame because of what You did for me. You know me, and You understand me when no one else does. When I follow You, I know I am on the right path. I love that You bend down to listen while I pray just like a father would bend down to hear his child. Daddy, praying to You is the best part of my day. Thank You for taking the time to listen. Help me live in the wholeness and freedom of Your presence.

If you don't have an earthly father you can trust, it might be hard to picture that you have a Heavenly Father who will never leave you or forsake you. If you have an earthly father who is too busy for you, it might be hard to picture that God wants to bend down and get closer to you just to listen to you. Psalms shows us over and over again that God wants you to run to Him and tell Him everything! He can't wait to talk to you. You can trust Him.

How do you view your relationship with God? Are you excited to talk to Him or afraid? Does God seem close or too far away to hear you?

Take a moment to pray, asking God to help you view Him like a loving father who cares about every detail of your life. He isn't waiting to punish you for what you have done wrong. He is waiting to redeem and rescue you.

What do you need to talk to God about today? Write it here and picture a Heavenly Father bending close to hear what you have to say!

Now picture your Heavenly Daddy hugging you and saying, "I heard you. I understand."

Day 25

When I feel **NERVOUS** . . .
I'm *victorious*

When I was in middle school, I started keeping a journal of my thoughts, questions, and prayers to God. It was my way of having a personal relationship with God. I would express whatever I was dealing with—the good, the bad, and the ugly—and keep track of all the many ways God responded to me and provided for me. It made my relationship with God feel more real when I put it in writing.

No one else knew I was doing this. I was very private. After my accident, my mom found all of my journals hidden under my bed. She was sort of shocked that I had been developing this intimate love relationship with God but never really talked openly about it. Today, I am grateful to have a record of what God and I were doing together during my early teenage years. I even have a journal I wrote to my future husband! I can't wait to give that to him when I meet him.

The other day I found this prayer I wrote to God right before I started high school. Evidently, I was pretty nervous. Wanna read my secret journal?

> Dear God,
>
> Starting high school gives me a brand-new start. I'm excited but also nervous because I'm the youngest. Do I really have what it takes? I'm not sure I'm ready. God, give me the courage to stand up and be an example to the older kids. Father, I know that even the "smallest" person can be used to change eternity. I want to be that person, and I am willing to do what it takes.

Nerves aren't really about courage or the lack of it. Nerves have everything to do with what you are focused on. On-the-way-to-high-school me was looking at all the older upperclassman and feeling intimidated, so of course I was nervous.

You probably have some things you feel nervous about. Maybe certain people make you nervous when you are around them. Maybe you are nervous about your grades or making a sports team. Maybe you are nervous to speak in public, and you have a big presentation coming up. Whatever it is that makes you nervous, chances are you are looking horizontally at people around you instead of looking up vertically at God.

When I was growing up, my pastor used to say, "Stop telling God how big your problems are, and start telling your problems how BIG your God is."

God has already given you the victory over everything you are nervous about. You just have to fix your eyes on Him and not focus on the thing that makes you nervous. Feeling nervous is totally normal. That nervous feeling reminds you to run to God and focus more on Him.

> **"Stop telling God how big your problems are, and start telling your problems how BIG your God is."**

One thing I love to do is color! I have tons of coloring books. When I first came out of the coma, I was blind and couldn't see color. I couldn't even see my mom or my dad. Every day now, I thank God for my eyesight and I stop and truly notice the colors around me. Have you ever noticed that God painted the sky blue and the grass green because those are the *calming* colors? The next time you feel nervous, get a big blanket and go lie outside, look at the sky, and talk to God. Get yourself looking up to God instead of at everything around you that might make you nervous. Let the words of Psalm 62 calm the waters of your heart.

Hint: Try bringing your favorite snack and your favorite drink, and make it a Victory Tea Party!

I WAIT QUIETLY BEFORE GOD,
 FOR MY VICTORY COMES FROM HIM.
HE ALONE IS MY ROCK AND MY SALVATION,
 MY FORTRESS WHERE I WILL NEVER BE SHAKEN.

PSALM 62:1–8

Almighty God,

When I am nervous, I'm not believing in Your power. When my hands are shaking or my heart is pounding, I can wait patiently for You to come to my rescue. I am waiting for the best answer, the best possible outcome. You are my healer and my deliverer. I give all of my "What ifs" to You. I don't have to be nervous about my future or about the next hour at school. You hold my future in the palm of Your hands.

LET ALL THAT I AM WAIT QUIETLY BEFORE GOD,
   FOR MY HOPE IS IN HIM.
HE ALONE IS MY ROCK AND MY SALVATION,
   MY FORTRESS WHERE I WILL NOT BE SHAKEN.

Understanding Father,

Thank You that I can talk to You all through my day. You are my secure rock. I can cling to You and give all my nerves to You. Calm the waters in my heart if I am applying too much pressure on myself. Thank You for giving me a sound mind instead of a spirit of fear. You are my protector and my provider.

MY VICTORY AND HONOR COME FROM GOD ALONE.

HE IS MY REFUGE, A ROCK WHERE NO ENEMY CAN REACH ME.

O MY PEOPLE, TRUST IN HIM AT ALL TIMES.

POUR OUT YOUR HEART TO HIM,

FOR GOD IS OUR REFUGE.

Prince of Peace,

Thank You for the confidence and the peace of knowing that the victory is always greater than the battle. One day I will see that it was all worth it. Father, help me trust in You alone and take the next step forward because with You all things are possible.

Take this action step: write these verses on a sticky note. Keep it by your bed, and quote it out loud every day for a week. Watch your nerves melt into victory.

I WAIT QUIETLY BEFORE GOD,

FOR MY VICTORY COMES FROM HIM.

HE ALONE IS MY ROCK AND MY SALVATION,

MY FORTRESS WHERE I WILL NEVER BE SHAKEN.

PSALM 62:1–8

173

Day 26

When I feel **STRESSED** . . .
I'm *being led* to a calmer place

Dear Lover of My Soul,

Peace is Your gift to me. You don't promise
that life will be easy, but You promise to
walk with me. When I try to do things in
my own strength, I'm stressed and overwhelmed because my focus is all about
me. But when I rely on Your unlimited
strength, that's when life is worth pushing
through. That's when I see You at work!
When I am weak, You are strong. When I
am weak, You get all the glory. When I am
weak, people don't see me, they see Jesus.
Father, give me supernatural peace today.
Lead me to a calmer place.

THE LORD IS MY SHEPHERD;

    I HAVE ALL THAT I NEED.

HE LETS ME REST IN GREEN MEADOWS;

    HE LEADS ME BESIDE PEACEFUL STREAMS.

HE RENEWS MY STRENGTH.

HE GUIDES ME ALONG RIGHT PATHS,

    BRINGING HONOR TO HIS NAME.

EVEN WHEN I WALK

    THROUGH THE DARKEST VALLEY,

I WILL NOT BE AFRAID,

    FOR YOU ARE CLOSE BESIDE ME.

YOUR ROD AND YOUR STAFF

    PROTECT AND COMFORT ME.

YOU PREPARE A FEAST FOR ME

    IN THE PRESENCE OF MY ENEMIES.

YOU HONOR ME BY ANOINTING MY HEAD WITH OIL.

    MY CUP OVERFLOWS WITH BLESSINGS.

SURELY YOUR GOODNESS AND UNFAILING LOVE WILL PURSUE ME

    ALL THE DAYS OF MY LIFE,

AND I WILL LIVE IN THE HOUSE OF THE LORD

    FOREVER.

Let's have a quick game of Truth or Dare!

Truth: Be totally honest. Did you just skip reading the Bible verses because you are really busy today? Thought you'd just fly through this devo to mark it off your list? If you did, you aren't the only one, but you probably are one of the ones who needs to read it twice, and let it soak into your soul!

Just ask Alexa or your internet browser. Both will tell you that teenagers are busier and facing more pressures today than ever before—yet at the same time getting less sleep and rest. As a result, more of your friends are being diagnosed with anxiety disorders than ever before. Do you think that is what God wants for you? Go back and read Psalm 23 again!

God Himself took a day to rest after six days of creative genius. We think of rest as taking a nap, but God doesn't sleep (Ps. 121:4). Rest is an action, an intentional choice to take a break and trust God to make up the difference. Rest is one of the Ten Commandments. Remember the Sabbath day? In the Old Testament farming culture, no work = no food. By following the Sabbath-day commandment, God's people were choosing to give up a day of work and trusting that God would provide. It was like saying, "God, I believe You can do more for me than I can do for me."

God made us with the need to rest so we would need more of Him. He wanted us to have a reason to run to Him.

When you feel stressed, that's not a bad thing. It's just a warning light (like a car's gas light warning that it's time to fill up the tank) that it's time to run to Jesus, and let Him fill you up with His peace and strength (which, by the way, can absolutely include taking a nap).

You might need to take a break from social media for an hour to enjoy God's creation. Talk to Him. Stare at the stars. Turn your problems over to Him. You might need to take a break from homework for an hour to be creative and do something you love. Go for a walk. Exercise. Sing in the shower. Dance in your room.

When we don't have margin and rest in our lives, it hinders our creativity, hinders our accomplishments, and hinders our relationship with God. His way of getting more done is by encouraging us to rest! That's how our amazing God works! He works on your behalf while you take a break and trust Him to make up the difference.

Dare: Do you know what STRESSED spells backward? Yeah, girl! As a tried-and true-chocolate lover, I can assure you that a little bit of DESSERTS every now and then actually helps the soul! Go find your favorite sweet or salty snack, and take a five-minute break to listen to your favorite praise song. Close your eyes to all the stress of life and open your eyes to Jesus. Give Him a solid five minutes to refill your soul and lead you to a calmer place.

Day 27

When I feel **TEMPTED** . . .
I'm too *valuable* for trouble

Imagine you had an unlimited amount of money to spend on one dress. What would it look like—a fantasy prom dress or your someday wedding dress? Visualize it. Would it be full and flowing like Cinderella's? Sleek and sparkly like a gown from the Miss America pageant? Or elegant and timeless like something Audrey Hepburn would've worn? What color would it be? How about the style? What material and accessories would you choose? Is it beautiful? I bet it is!

Draw a picture of your dream dress here, or if you don't like to draw, describe it in writing:

Now imagine wearing your priceless dream dress in a mud pen to catch a greased pig. Would it make any sense to ruin something so valuable and perfect, tailored just for you? That's how God feels about us when we fall into sin. We are His dwelling place, His palace, His treasure of great price. He longs to protect us from being damaged or wounded.

During the next few years, you will face many new and exciting temptations. I hope you know how much your Heavenly Father longs to shield you. He inspired Psalm 141 specifically to help us overcome temptation. Let's read and pray this psalm together. (If you have a godly friend you trust, try reading and praying this psalm with your friend sometime too!)

PSALM 141:3–10 NIV

SET A GUARD OVER MY MOUTH, LORD;
    KEEP WATCH OVER THE DOOR OF MY LIPS.
DO NOT LET MY HEART BE DRAWN TO WHAT IS EVIL
    SO THAT I TAKE PART IN WICKED DEEDS
ALONG WITH THOSE WHO ARE EVILDOERS;
    DO NOT LET ME EAT THEIR DELICACIES.

Dear Protector,

There is so much temptation in this world today. I feel it every moment, and I don't want to give in. Father, please strengthen me through the Holy Spirit, and fill me with discernment. Burn a passion within

my heart that wants to serve You alone. I
don't want to weaken my faith or quench
the Spirit by giving in to sinful desires.
Lord, I know my mouth can be used for
good or for evil. Help me think before I
speak and only say words that will build up
people and speak life. Keep my mind pure
and my eyes focused on You.

MY EYES ARE FIXED ON YOU, SOVEREIGN LORD;
    IN YOU I TAKE REFUGE—DO NOT GIVE ME OVER TO DEATH.
KEEP ME SAFE FROM THE TRAPS SET BY EVILDOERS,
    FROM THE SNARES THEY HAVE LAID FOR ME.
LET THE WICKED FALL INTO THEIR OWN NETS,
    WHILE I PASS BY IN SAFETY.

Dear Holy One,

Give me Your power to overcome any
scheme or trap of the deceiver. Help me
take every thought captive and recognize
Satan's lies that fill me with shame and
leave me feeling unworthy, useless, and
unloved. I refuse to believe those lies.
I am believing the truth that You, Lord,

are my redeemer, my advocate, and my best friend. When I am tempted, help me remember that I am Your dwelling place. My body is Your temple. The King of kings and Lord of lords lives inside of me. Wow! That is an unspeakable honor. Help me run to You when I am tempted! You are always waiting for me with open arms. You are my refuge and my shield. Guard my heart and mind and body. Thank You for doing battle for my heart, Jesus. You are my champion!

Day 28

When I feel **TIRED** . . .
I'm *relying* on God's strength

If you could have an unlimited gift card for any store, which one would you pick?

What are the first five things you would buy with your unlimited spending power?

1. _____

2. _____

3. _____

4. _____

5. _____

It's fun to think about living "unlimited" because we are all limited by our human nature. We can only go about three weeks without food, three days without water, three minutes without air (and maybe even less than that without our favorite store!). Our human bodies are limited in strength. We require sleep and bathroom breaks and sleep and lunch breaks and sleep!

How many hours did you sleep last night? Do you know that if you live to be seventy-five and you get an average of eight hours of sleep at night, you will spend twenty-five years of your life sleeping? It's a good thing God never sleeps and that He is working things out for us while we sleep.

But what about when you need to be awake and wish you were asleep? In spite of sleeping one-third of your life, you're at an age when you are growing physically, emotionally, and spiritually, which is all pretty exhausting. Add to that the pressures of school, sports, a social life, and other activities, and I'm guessing you have a lot of days when you feel tired.

God is all-powerful. His strength is unlimited. And guess what? If you belong to Him, His Spirit lives inside you, which means His supernatural power is accessible to you 24/7. Psalm 18:29 says, "In [God's] strength I can crush an army; with my God, I can scale any wall." Sounds pretty unlimited to me! Wouldn't it be fun to live that way?

You can choose to rely on God's unlimited strength instead of your limited supply. His strength works best when you are feeling weak. All you have to do is ask Him for help. God's power becomes our power through prayer. *Asking* is where the power happens. Ask God to unleash His power in you.

When I was fifteen, I would set my alarm thirty minutes earlier than I needed to get up in order to spend time reading God's Word and journaling my thoughts to Him before school. It was the best part of my day. I would sit in my big, lime-green chair and spend time with Him. God was my safe place. He was the only One I could share my heart and my deepest thoughts with. God would speak to my heart, and I would write what He said to me. You would think this would make me more tired because I was getting less sleep, but it actually gave me *more* energy, strength, and courage for the day.

So take this challenge: For one week, try setting your alarm fifteen-to-thirty minutes earlier to spend time with God. See if you have more energy after tapping into His unlimited power.

How can you spend time with God? One way is to read a few verses and reply to God with a prayer from your heart, like we've been learning to do together.

IN YOUR STRENGTH I CAN CRUSH AN ARMY;
WITH MY GOD I CAN SCALE ANY WALL.

Father,

Unleash Your strength on my life. I embrace
Your power today instead of my own.
With the King of kings on my side, I
can do anything! Thank You for doing
the impossible through me!

GOD'S WAY IS PERFECT.
ALL THE LORD'S PROMISES PROVE TRUE.

Jesus,

Your yoke is easy, and Your burden is light.
Your way is being strong when I am weak.
Thank You for raising me up and healing me.
I trust Your promises. Today I am relying on
You to (FILL IN YOUR NEEDS HERE):

HE IS A SHIELD FOR ALL WHO LOOK TO HIM FOR
   PROTECTION.
FOR WHO IS GOD EXCEPT THE LORD?
   WHO BUT OUR GOD IS A SOLID ROCK?

Holy Spirit,

You are the best at comforting me. I just
want to say thank You for being my solid
rock. Honestly, today, I'm too tired to
know what I should pray. Would You help
me pray? Thank You for always being there
for me!

GOD ARMS ME WITH STRENGTH,
   AND HE MAKES MY WAY PERFECT.
HE MAKES ME AS SUREFOOTED AS A DEER,
   ENABLING ME TO STAND ON MOUNTAIN HEIGHTS.

We have one God in three persons—God the Father,
God the Son, and God the Holy Spirit. God the Father,
who created me and holds the whole universe in the palm
of His hand, sent His Son, Jesus, to earth to die on the
cross for me and pay the penalty for my sins. Since Jesus
was once in human flesh, He understands every feeling

I will ever experience because He experienced them too. The moment I receive Jesus as my Savior, the Holy Spirit comes to live *in* me. The Holy Spirit is my Comforter and Guide. The Holy Spirit convicts me of sin and helps me know right from wrong. You may have noticed that sometimes I like to pray to each person of the Trinity individually because each has a different role in my life.

Try writing in your own prayer here in response to the verses you just read.

Dear Father (my Creator),

_____

_____

_____

_____

Dear Jesus (my Redeemer),

_____

_____

_____

_____

I'M *relying* ON GOD'S STRENGTH

Dear Holy Spirit (my Guide),

_____

_____

_____

_____

YOU HAVE GIVEN ME YOUR SHIELD OF VICTORY.
    YOUR RIGHT HAND SUPPORTS ME;
    YOUR HELP HAS MADE ME GREAT.
YOU HAVE MADE A WIDE PATH FOR MY FEET
    TO KEEP THEM FROM SLIPPING.

Lord,

I'm begging You to use me to impact and encourage others. I want to help people smile. I want my life to shout to others that there is hope. Fill me with Your unlimited strength so I can do everything You have planned for me today. I pray that I would carry a hint of Your glory today and reflect how great You are. I surrender all of my strength for Your strength.

Day 29

When I feel **UGLY** ...
I'm *wonderfully* made

Have you ever made a wish that went something like this: *I wish I had straighter hair, longer legs, eyes of a different color, a smaller nose*? Or how about this: *I wish I were smarter, faster, funnier, better at making friends*? How much time do you think you have spent looking in the mirror or staring at your selfies wishing for something you don't see there?

Guess what? It might surprise you that God spends way more time thinking about you than you spend thinking about yourself. He wrote a song for you in Psalm 139 that says He thinks about you more than there are grains of sand on all the ocean floors combined. Wow! That's a lot of thoughts about you!

This song tells us that God is marveling at how amazing you are. That's right. He loves every single thing about you. In fact, He created you. Your Heavenly Father handpicked your personality and your unique talents. There is no one exactly like you. God has an extraordinary plan for your life that only you can fulfill.

Check out the song He wrote for you.

FOR YOU CREATED MY INMOST BEING;
YOU KNIT ME TOGETHER IN MY MOTHER'S WOMB.
I PRAISE YOU BECAUSE I AM FEARFULLY AND WONDERFULLY MADE;
    YOUR WORKS ARE WONDERFUL,
    I KNOW THAT FULL WELL.

PSALM 139:13–18 NIV

Dear Creator God,

Wow! Just to think that I have a Creator gives me chills. You chose what color my eyes would be, and You could hear the sound of my laughter echoing in Your heart before I was ever born. You called me Yours even before time began! It is so cool to know I was created to reflect who You are. Please help me remember that I

am fearfully and wonderfully made. Forgive
me for the times when I look at myself in
shame or wish I could change what You
have created.

MY FRAME WAS NOT HIDDEN FROM YOU
    WHEN I WAS MADE IN THE SECRET PLACE,
    WHEN I WAS WOVEN TOGETHER IN THE DEPTHS OF
      THE EARTH.
YOUR EYES SAW MY UNFORMED BODY;
    ALL THE DAYS ORDAINED FOR ME WERE WRITTEN IN
      YOUR BOOK
    BEFORE ONE OF THEM CAME TO BE.
HOW PRECIOUS TO ME ARE YOUR THOUGHTS, GOD!
    HOW VAST IS THE SUM OF THEM!
WERE I TO COUNT THEM,
    THEY WOULD OUTNUMBER THE GRAINS OF SAND.

Father,

You handcrafted every detail of my body
and personality so there would be no one
else like me. I am one-of-a-kind! No one

else can fulfill the amazing plan You have
for me. I am unique! I am beautiful! I am
Yours. There is no replica of me. To think
you love me that much is just amazing!
Lord, thank You that there are no acci-
dents in Your book. You designed every
single day of my life according to Your
perfect will and plan. Daddy, my desire
is to shine for You. I don't want to look
down on myself or wish I were a copy of
someone else. Help me see myself through
Your eyes and not compare myself to
others. I'm so honored to be a daughter of
the King.

Now it's your turn. Try writing your own prayer to God. Imagine Psalm 139:17–18 (paraphrased) are God's text message to you: "I can't stop thinking about you. You make me smile constantly. I think of you *more* times than there are grains of sand on the ocean floor!" What would you text back to Him? There are no right or wrong words. Just write the first thing that pops into your mind. He loves your thoughts! Write your reply on the next page:

Day 30

When I feel **UNPOPULAR** ...
I'm made to *stand out*

I don't blend in. I have a brain injury. I stand out, but I love standing out and standing up for what really matters. I don't want to fit in. I want to make a difference!

Define *popular*. Seriously, what does *popular* actually mean?

Did you know that many dictionaries offer two definitions of *popular*? The first says something like, "what everybody admires, likes, or desires to be." The second definition might surprise you. It goes something like this: "generic, non-special, middle-of-the-road."

Do you really want to be generic, non-special, and just like everyone else when you were made to be SO MUCH MORE? You were never meant to fit into the world; you were made to change it! You were never designed to make your name great. You were created to make God's name great. That can only happen when you are brave enough to be YOU!

Stop trying to blend into everything around you, and start making a difference in everyone around you! Here's how.

PSALM 138:1–8

I GIVE YOU THANKS, O LORD, WITH ALL MY HEART;
    I WILL SING YOUR PRAISES BEFORE THE GODS.
I BOW BEFORE YOUR HOLY TEMPLE AS I WORSHIP.
        I PRAISE YOUR NAME FOR YOUR UNFAILING LOVE
            AND FAITHFULNESS;
FOR YOUR PROMISES ARE BACKED
        BY ALL THE HONOR OF YOUR NAME.

Lord,

It's okay if I'm not in the popular crowd because I don't want to blend in. I want to stand out and be a LIGHT for You in the darkness—because people are drawn to the light. The psalmist calls Your Word "a lamp to guide my feet and a light for my path" (Ps. 119:105). When there is light to illuminate the path, we can see the potential dangers in front of us and walk another way. I know if I'm willing to stand up and be different, others will follow. Help me obey Your Word!

AS SOON AS I PRAY, YOU ANSWER ME;
YOU ENCOURAGE ME BY GIVING ME STRENGTH.

Dear Hope-Giver,

I have to smile because You call out the exact opposite of who we are in our own strength. Thank You for reminding me of the story in Your Word when Gideon was hiding, and You called him a "mighty warrior." If we are shy, You can give us passion to shine for You. If we are afraid, You can give

us courage. If we are insecure, You can
give us confidence. If we don't feel smart,
You can give us Your wisdom.

THOUGH THE LORD IS GREAT, HE CARES FOR THE HUMBLE,
    BUT HE KEEPS HIS DISTANCE FROM THE PROUD.

THOUGH I AM SURROUNDED BY TROUBLES,
    YOU WILL PROTECT ME FROM THE ANGER OF MY ENEMIES.
YOU REACH OUT YOUR HAND,
    AND THE POWER OF YOUR RIGHT HAND SAVES ME.

Dear Faithful One,

Thank You for Your unfailing love. When
I cry out to You, I know You will answer.
Father, I am grateful You see me in my
lowliness, but You don't leave me there.
You call out the BOLDNESS in me. Lord,
I know You don't use the proud. You use
the humble instead. Thank You that in my
weakness, You are strong. There is HOPE
for me because You delight in using the
incapable for Your glory. So that means
You can use me just as I am.

THE LORD WILL WORK OUT HIS PLANS FOR MY LIFE—
FOR YOUR FAITHFUL LOVE, O LORD, ENDURES FOREVER.
DON'T ABANDON ME, FOR YOU MADE ME.

Daddy,

Thank You for seeing the BEST in me. I am
so grateful You preserve my life, and You
will fulfill the purpose You ordained for me
since before the beginning of time. I have
nothing to fear because Your right hand
will protect me and guide me. I like who I
am, but I get excited about the potential of
who I could be. I'm going to stop blending
in and start changing the world!

What is one change you might make so you can be a
light at school or around your friends? Try drawing a
picture of it. While you are doodling, ask God to give
you His picture of what He wants your life to look like.
Try praying, *God, show me what You want me to be like
this year.*

Priceless

A PERSONAL NOTE FROM JEN

Sometimes I wish my life were a book and I could skip ahead a couple of chapters to find out what happens: Will I ever get married? Will God heal my eyes so I can drive a car? Will I have children one day? But then I hear God whisper softly, JEN, YOU CAN TRUST ME. I HAD YOUR WHOLE LIFE PLANNED OUT BEFORE YOU WERE EVER BORN.

The beauty is in the trusting. I'm on an adventure with God. Doctors gave me no hope. They thought I would never walk, talk, read, or write again. But God delights in doing the impossible! He is the author of my story, and I can trust that His plan is best. You can trust Him too.

God has a very special purpose for your life. He has planned something only you can do. He can use you right now at a young age to be a light for Him. You can pray every morning, "Lord, I don't want to miss one plan You have for me today."

Close your eyes right now and picture yourself crawling up into the lap of your Heavenly Father. As He wraps His loving arms around you, may you know that His Word tells you that:

I am so proud of you, and My plan for your life is way bigger and greater than anything you could dream possible.

You are beautiful,

You are PRICELESS,

You are Mine.

P.S. I would love to hear your story. You can connect with me on social media at hopeoutloud.com or email Jen@hopeoutloud.com.

ACKNOWLEDGMENTS

A huge thank you to my aunt Christy Murphy

for helping my mom and me write, organize, and
make this book a reality.

I also greatly appreciate my cousins
Allie and Ashley Murphy, who inspired me
to write this book so that girls their age
could find their true worth and value
in the arms of Jesus.

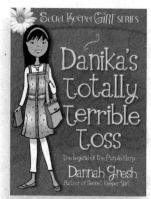
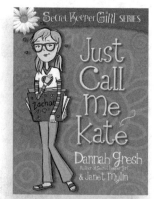
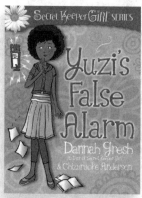
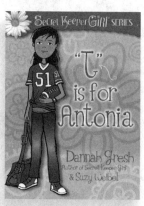

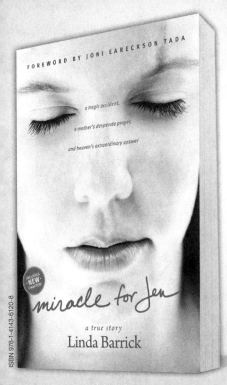